THE
TRANSCONTINENTAL
RAILROAD

THE GATEWAY TO THE WEST

MILESTONES
IN
AMERICAN HISTORY

THE TREATY OF PARIS

THE MONROE DOCTRINE

THE TRANSCONTINENTAL RAILROAD

THE ELECTRIC LIGHT

THE WRIGHT BROTHERS

THE STOCK MARKET CRASH OF 1929

SPUTNIK/EXPLORER I

THE CIVIL RIGHTS ACT OF 1964

MILESTONES
IN
AMERICAN HISTORY

THE TRANSCONTINENTAL RAILROAD

THE GATEWAY TO THE WEST

EDWARD J. RENEHAN JR.

CHELSEA HOUSE
PUBLISHERS

An imprint of Infobase Publishing

Cover: Workers celebrate after the final rail spike is driven into the ground at Promontory Summit, Utah, on May 10, 1869.

The Transcontinental Railroad: The Gateway to the West

Copyright © 2007 by Infobase Publishing

Chelsea House
An imprint of Infobase Publishing
132 West 31st Street
New York, NY 10001

ISBN 10: 0-7910-9351-4
ISBN 13: 978-0-7910-9351-1

Library of Congress Cataloging-in-Publication Data
Renehan, Edward, 1956-
  The Transcontinental Railroad : the gateway to the West / Edward J. Renehan, Jr.
     p. cm. — (Milestones in American history)
  Includes bibliographical references and index.
  ISBN 0–7910–9351–4 (hardcover)
  1. Railroads—United States—History—19th century—Juvenile literature. 2. Central Pacific Railroad Company—History—Juvenile literature. 3. Union Pacific Railroad Company—History—Juvenile literature. 4. West (U.S.)—History. I. Title. II. Series.
  TF25.U5R465 2007
  385.0979—dc22   2006038870

Series design by Erik Lindstrom
Cover design by Ben Peterson

Printed in the United States of America

Bang NMSG 10 9 8 7 6 5 4 3 2 1

This book is printed on acid-free paper.

All links and Web addresses were checked and verified to be correct at the time of publication. Because of the dynamic nature of the Web, some addresses and links may have changed since publication and may no longer be valid.

CONTENTS

Gold, Silver, and Iron Spikes

Today, an unusual park—the Golden Spike National Historic Site, administered by the National Park Service—is located at what was once the town of Promontory, at Promontory Summit in Utah, 32 miles west of Brigham City. It was at Promontory Summit that—on May 10, 1869—two trains met and several spikes (two golden spikes from California, one silver spike from Nevada, one iron spike with silver and gold plating from Arizona, and one simple iron spike that was left in place thereafter) were positioned in a ceremonial railroad tie to symbolically "complete" a marvelous feat of engineering.

The Transcontinental Railway, known in its day also as the Pacific Railway, was the first to link America's Atlantic and Pacific coasts. Here at Promontory, the Union Pacific's coal-burning *Engine No. 119* (aimed west) and the Central Pacific's wood-burning *Jupiter* (aimed east) touched cowcatchers—the slanted metal frame at the front of each engine—to signify the uniting of the country through the enterprising application of industrial science. But today the two most important relics of that historic joining of the continent's eastern and western shores no longer exist. *Engine 119* went to the scrap yard in 1903, and the *Jupiter* followed suit in 1909. As of 1904, most trains began avoiding Promontory altogether, after a new and better adjacent line was launched amid easier country. Then, in 1942, the Union Pacific held an "Undriving of the Last Spike" ceremony, immediately before ripping up 90 miles of track: all of it destined for metal scrap to be used in the World War II effort. This "Undriving" ceremony was an irony that no one participating in the grand events of May 10, 1869, could have foreseen.

CALIFORNIA'S PREMATURE CELEBRATION

It was a little before 9 A.M. on the morning of May 10, 1869, when the Union Pacific train pulled up at Promontory. "We went over at once to greet them," wrote one of the officials who accompanied Central Pacific official Leland Stanford. "In a superb piece of cabinet-work they call a 'Pullman car,' we met [Union Pacific] Vice President [Thomas C.] Durant, of whom we have heard so much, with a black velvet coat and gay necktie, that seemed to have been the 'last tie' to which he had been giving his mind, gorgeously gotten up. General [Grenville] Dodge was there, and he looked like business. The veterans [Sidney] Dillon and [John] Duff [both of the Union Pacific] were there to give away the bride. General Dodge on the part of the Union Pacific, and Edgar Mills on the part of the Central Pacific, were appointed to arrange the preliminaries."

Everything between the Central Pacific and the Union Pacific had, for years, been the subject of jealous competition and intense negotiation. Each firm had struggled at breakneck speed to gain the most miles of track in the American West. Starting from California, the Central Pacific had wanted the place of meeting between the two companies to be as far east

One of the prominent figures in organizing the construction of the Transcontinental Railroad was Leland Stanford. The California native served as governor of his home state from 1861 to 1863 and became president of the Central Pacific Railroad in 1861.

as possible. Starting from the Missouri River, the men of the Union Pacific preferred laying down ties as far west as possible. The two rival companies wound up meeting 1,086 miles west of the Missouri and 960 miles east of Sacramento, California.

No one mentioned the untimely delay that had caused the Union Pacific party to arrive on the tenth, as opposed to the eighth, as originally planned. On the eighth, when Durant's train passed through Piedmont, Utah, it had been stopped and seized by disgruntled railway construction workers. The workers boarded the train and surrounded Durant. They told him they were hungry and must have the money they had been promised for their labor, and they warned him that they would detain him until those funds were forthcoming. This was a sign of what was to come, as both railroads eventually reneged on debts going forward. But for the moment, Durant made good on what he owed the construction crews, and within a day he was allowed to move on.

The drama at Piedmont led to premature celebrations in San Francisco and Sacramento, where parties were well under-way before word of the delay came through via telegraph. "The Pacific Railroad celebration today was one to be remembered for all time in San Francisco," wrote a reporter for one of that town's newspapers. He continued:

> The day was ushered in by a salute of 100 guns. All the federal forts of the harbor fired a salute, the city bells were rung, and steam whistles blown. At night, the whole city was illuminated and presented a brilliant appearance. The procession was the largest and most enthusiastic ever witnessed in San Francisco. The people were eager and willing to observe an event of so much importance to this city and the Pacific coast, and turned out en masse. Business was generally suspended. Nearly every citizen exhibited a hearty interest in the demonstration. The military and civic display was grand. In addition to the state military, all the available United States

troops from the several forts here participated on the occasion, while the civic societies turned out with full ranks.

In Sacramento, citizens from that city and those who came in from nearby Nevada converged by the thousands. As the *New York Times* reported: "The lines of travel to and from Sacramento were thrown open to the public free and immense numbers of people took advantage of the circumstances and flocked thither. The Central Pacific Company had thirty locomotives gaily decked and ranged in front of the city, and as the signal gun was fired announcing the driving of the last spike of the road the locomotives opened a chorus of whistles, and all the bells and steam whistles in the city joined in." But the organizers of the celebrations in Sacramento and San Francisco—the two cities destined to benefit more than any other California towns from the new railroad—were soon pronounced wrong in their assumption that the golden spike ceremony had come off as and when planned. The same *New York Times* reporter noted that at the end of the day, "profound regret" was expressed because "the roads were not joined." But the delay would only be two days.

CEREMONIAL SPIKES

On May 10, the day the ceremonial spikes would finally be nailed down, the Irish and Chinese immigrant laborers who had built much of the railroad in either direction mingled amicably with local Mormons who had proved critical in the final stages of the work. Only the Chinese and the Irish, however, gave any trade to the liquor sellers who set up their tents and did a brisk business. All the Mormons abstained. Meanwhile, the Chinese and Irish drank toasts to celebratory background music provided by the Tenth Ward Band of Ogden, Utah.

Late in the morning, a small crew of Central Pacific workers was put to work leveling the last remaining patch of soil between the two extensions of rail and laying down the ties. As they worked, Leland Stanford's private railroad car, pulled by the *Jupiter*, inched closer up the track. "From this train," writes historian David Howard Bain in his book *Empire Express*, "men carried one last ceremonial tie: donated by a now well-heeled contractor and prepared by a San Francisco billiard-table manufacturer, it was cut from a California laurel on Mount Tamalpais, sawed into an eight-foot length, eight inches by eight around and polished until it reflected light, and it bore a silver plate identifying it as the last tie of the Pacific railroad, followed by the names of the directors and officers of the Central Pacific, and the presenter, West Evans."

Mr. Evans could well afford the grandiose gesture. As a contractor who supplied most of the Central Pacific ties, he— like so many other contractors employed by both the Central Pacific and the Union Pacific—had made a killing through inflated prices in no-bid contracts, aggressively milking the generous grants extended by the federal government to each company engaged in the creation of the Transcontinental Railroad. Eventually, there would be congressional investigations and even a suicide. But all that was in the vague future on the day of celebration, when the spikes finally went into the earth.

Inside one of the railroad cars owned by the Union Pacific, representatives of the two companies quibbled over which president, Durant or Stanford, should wield the hammer driving down the final spike. Finally, after much rancor, it was agreed that Stanford would stand on the eastern side of the spike and strike the first blow, while Durant, standing on the western side, would deliver a follow-up pounding. Concurrent with these ceremonies, telegraph operators were poised to apprise waiting crowds in Chicago, New York, Boston, San Francisco, and Sacramento of the final triumph.

At around 2:27 P.M., telegraph operator Watson Shilling at Promontory Summit used Morse code to tap out a message for

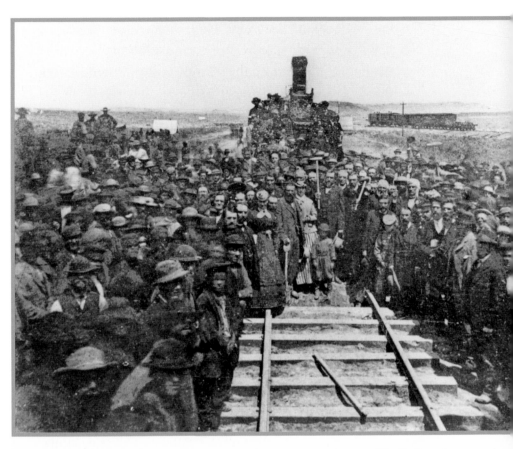

After about four years of work, construction on the Union Pacific Railroad was completed at Promontory, Utah, on May 10, 1869. Pictured here are railway workers who are preparing to celebrate the historic event, which linked nearly 1,800 miles (2,897 kilometers) of track between Omaha, Nebraska, and Sacramento, California.

the world: "Almost ready. Hats off. Prayer is being offered." And then at 2:40 P.M.: "We have got done praying. Spike is about to be presented." After that, the telegraphic listeners across the continent were in for a long wait, as the various spikes were ceremoniously presented, and Stanford made lengthy remarks accepting the gifts. "The Pacific Railroad accepts with pride and satisfaction these golden and silver tokens of your appreciation of the importance of our enterprise," said Stanford, "[to the] material interest of the whole country, East and West, North and South. These gifts shall receive a fitting place in the superstructure of our road. Before laying the tie and driving the spikes, in the completion of the Pacific Railway, allow me to express the hope that the great importance which you are pleased to attach to our undertaking may be in all respects fully realized." About a half hour of silence dominated the telegraph lines before telegraph operator W. N. Shilling finally sent the message: "All ready now, the spike will soon be driven. The signal will be three dots for the commencement of the blows." A moment later, as Durant and Stanford stood with hammers poised, Stanford's hammer began to fall and Shilling typed out the dots.

The golden spike was in fact never put into the ground: The soft gold would never have absorbed the blows without becoming deformed. Once the two lines were connected, Durant and Stanford shook hands. Durant announced, "There is henceforth but one Pacific Railroad of the United States." After that, the two men stepped away to safety, and the two engines nosed slowly toward one another. A few moments later, with their cowcatchers nearly touching, the engineers climbed to the front of their engines and reached across to shake hands and clink champagne bottles together. Shortly thereafter, formal telegraph messages were sent to President Ulysses S. Grant, Vice President Schuyler Colfax, and other eminent persons, including General John A. Rawlins (secretary of war).

For the balance of the day in the Utah desert, the whiskey tents did a brisk business, while the few remaining sober workers—most of them Mormon—removed Evans's ornate ceremonial tie with its special spikes. At the same time, con men moved among the drinkers, signing them up for $5 charms supposedly to be struck from the gold in the golden spike—purchase price payable in advance. The Union Pacific's chief engineer, General Grenville Dodge—who, as a young man had met Abraham Lincoln at Council Bluffs, Iowa, in 1859 and first broached the subject of the Transcontinental Railroad with the future president—watched all this with a bemused smile.

CELEBRATIONS

Upon receipt of the message, merriment broke out throughout the nation. "This day has been one long to be remembered in the history of this city," chronicled a Chicago reporter. He continued:

> The demonstration in honor of the Pacific Railroad was a true uprising of the people, spontaneous and not manufactured to order. The city was all decorated with flags, banners, etc., and when bells announced that the last spike had been driven an immense procession began to move. Owing to its enormous length it was found impossible to adhere to the program, and the Marshals guided it as best they could. Apparently, nearly every vehicle in the city took part, and nearly the whole population turned out. Never were the streets of Chicago more densely packed. Business was totally suspended. . . . The bells were ringing, nearly all the steam whistles in the city sounded and cannon boomed forth congratulations over the great event.

Similar celebrations took place in other cities. Bells and whistles went off as soon as the signal from Utah was received. In New York, a gathering of citizens downtown embarked upon a civilized and restrained program of prayers and songs—but only after a hundred cannons in City Hall Park shook the windows of Lower Manhattan with their massive salute. At Philadelphia, the bell at Independence Hall sounded, as did the bells of every fire station in town. At Buffalo, New York, the large crowd gave three cheers, joined in a public prayer, and then sang the "Star Spangled Banner." In Washington, a clerk in the attorney general's office who fancied himself a poet could not get enough news of the railroad's completion. A few months later, the same clerk, Walt Whitman, would begin one of his famous efforts, "Passage to India," with the following lines celebrating both the Transcontinental Railroad and the telegraph:

> *Singing my days,*
> *Singing the great achievements of the present,*
> *Singing the strong, light works of engineers,*
> *Our modern wonders, (the antique ponderous Seven*
> * outvied,)*
> *In the Old World, the east, the Suez canal,*
> *The New by its mighty railroad spann'd,*
> *The seas inlaid with eloquent, gentle wires,*
> *I sound, to commence, the cry, with thee, O soul,*
> *The Past! the Past! the Past!*

Two Companies

It was a hot day in August 1859, when Abraham Lincoln—a candidate for the Republican Party's presidential nomination—came out from Illinois to Council Bluffs, Iowa, to give a speech. Among those in attendance that day was Grenville Mellen Dodge, 28 years old. Dodge was a brilliant engineer and local entrepreneur (engaged in banking, milling, merchandizing, contracting, and real estate) who was introduced to the candidate as knowing more about railroads than almost anyone else in the country. According to Dodge's own account of their subsequent conversation, Lincoln pointedly asked him, "Dodge, what's the best route for a Pacific railroad to the West?" To this Dodge answered, "From this town out the Platte Valley." Upon further quizzing from Lincoln, Dodge explained that the 42nd parallel (42° north latitude) of the map constituted the "most practical and economic" for the building of a transcontinental railroad, due to the uniform grade along the Platte River Valley to the point of the Rocky Mountains. Dodge added that Council Bluffs was the logical place of departure for the rail line to the Pacific, due to several railroads then building toward that spot from Chicago, with further links all the way back to New York and Boston. (Dodge later amended his recommended geography but only slightly. Once he realized rails extending out from Chicago were aimed at Omaha, he recommended this as the starting point.)

Dodge recalled answering Lincoln's pointed questions for an hour or more, until Lincoln had mined Dodge's insights to their fullest. "He shelled my woods completely," Dodge remembered, "and got all the information I'd collected." A few years later, during the summer of 1862, Congress would pass and Lincoln would sign the Pacific Railway Act, signaling the start of the race between the Central Pacific and Union Pacific railroads to build a transcontinental railroad connecting America's eastern and western coasts, and thus fulfilling the ideal of the concept called manifest destiny.

MANIFEST DESTINY

The concept of manifest destiny meant that it was obvious (manifest) and inevitable (destiny) that the young country would eventually expand across the North American continent, spreading democracy and culture from one ocean to the other. To many pundits, speculators, and politicians, the ideal tool of manifest destiny was the Transcontinental Railroad.

As historian Stephen Ambrose wrote in his book *Nothing Like It in the World*, "The Transcontinental Railroad had been talked about, promoted, encouraged, desired for three decades" before work actually commenced. As early as 1853, Congress had called for a study of proposed routes to the California coast. Then Secretary of War Jefferson Davis—future president of the Confederacy—sent out four teams of surveyors to explore four different possibilities: one to the north across the

After the discovery of gold in California in 1848, California's admission to statehood in 1850, and the boom in westward migration that resulted, President Franklin Pierce commissioned Secretary of War Jefferson Davis (pictured here) to explore the possibility of constructing a railway route to the West. In 1853, Davis directed four surveys of potential routes to the Pacific Ocean, none of which ended up being selected.

Dakotas and the northern Rockies near the Canadian border, one to the south near the Mexico border, and two in between. Eventually, railroads would be built in each of these regions. However, not one of Davis's teams investigated Dodge's ideal path: the 42nd parallel through the Platte Valley.

Grenville Dodge, the young man with whom Lincoln spoke in Council Bluffs, was a native of Massachusetts. Starting off as a surveyor for the Rock Island Railroad, he eventually studied engineering at Norwich University in Vermont. There, he developed a passion for the new twin technologies of railroading and steam power. A few lines the young man wrote in a diary entry from autumn 1850 put his excitement in context: "Forty-three years ago today, on October 12, 1807, [Robert] Fulton made his first steamboat trip up the Hudson River. How wonderful has been the effect of his discovery. In the short space of forty-three years steam power has revolutionized the world." Two years later, Dodge went to work for the Illinois Central, then in 1853 returned to the Rock Island, which he characterized in a letter to his father as "the true Pacific road [which] will be built to Council Bluffs and then on to San Francisco—this being the shortest and most feasible route." As Stephen Ambrose has observed, "Iowa was a natural link between the roads being pushed west from Chicago and any road crossing the Missouri River. When Chicago became a railroad center, Iowa became the necessary bridge between the Midwest and the Far West."

During 1853, Dodge—working for a subsidiary of the Rock Island called the Missouri & Mississippi Railroad—set out with 14 men to survey, in his own words, "the great Platte as far into Nebraska as we see fit." Eventually, he took out a claim on the Elkhorn River, the first major tributary to the Platte, some 20 miles west of Omaha, and moved there with his wife, but he later moved on to Council Bluffs. During 1856 and into 1857, Dodge mapped the Platte Valley to the Rockies, working for a group of investors headed by railroad entrepreneur Dr. Thomas Durant—a man with a medical degree who never practiced medicine, preferring to "operate" on Wall Street—and Durant's close associate in the Rock Island Railroad, Henry Farnum.

Durant and his group subsequently sought to interest Eastern financiers in extending track across Iowa, over the Missouri River, and into Nebraska. "On the basis of Dodge's reports," writes Ambrose, "they selected Council Bluffs as the place for the Rock Island to end and the Pacific railroad, when the government decided to build it, to begin. This was an adroit and far-seeing move . . . and it induced Dodge to make a claim across the Missouri River and near the town of Council Bluffs. Railroad activity was down, however, because of the Panic of 1857." Indeed, a financial depression that year brought much of the economy and infrastructure growth of the nation to a standstill for quite some time.

During the previous several decades, the growth of American railroads had been fast-paced. In fact, despite the Panic of 1857, an average of 2,160 miles of new track was laid in every year throughout the 1850s in the United States. What is more, the amount of track laid had more than doubled in each decade since the 1830s. In 1834, the country boasted approximately 762 miles of track; 10 years later, 4,311 miles; and 10 years after that, 15,675 miles. By 1858—when Dodge had his conversation with Lincoln—Dodge and other entrepreneurial men such as Durant and Farnum had firmly committed themselves to building a transcontinental railroad, by hook or by crook.

LAUNCHING THE PACIFIC ROAD

Shortly after the presidential election of 1860, but several months before Abraham Lincoln's inauguration in March 1861, a friend of Dodge's by the name of Peter Reed paid a courtesy call on Lincoln at his home in Springfield, Illinois. "I called his attention," Reed wrote Dodge, "to the needs of the people of Nebraska and the western slope of Iowa. I said to him that our interest had been badly neglected. I told him that I expected to see some men from Council Bluffs in regard to this matter and that you were one of them. He said that his sympathies were with the border people, as he was a border man himself. I think that we are all right with Mr. Lincoln."

Immediately after Lincoln's inauguration, Dodge and his associates were in Washington, D.C., lobbying for a Pacific railroad to run due west from Council Bluffs. Dodge himself attended the swearing in of the new president. "Old Abe delivered the greatest speech of the age," Dodge wrote his wife. "It is backbone all over." Elsewhere in the note he added: "It looks as though we can get all our measures through and then I'll make tracks for home." But Lincoln had other business with which he was immediately occupied. As Southern Confederates (those who wanted to withdraw from the Union) rattled their swords two weeks after the inaugural, Dodge called at the White House. "Politically the skies are dark," he wrote his wife. "Lincoln has a hard task before him, but he says that he thinks he can bring the country out all right." Two weeks after that, on April 12, while Dodge visited and did business in New York, Confederate forces fired on Fort Sumter in South Carolina, and the Civil War began. Soon Dodge enlisted in the Union Army. It would be more than a year before legislation launching the construction of the Pacific Railroad could be finalized—but Lincoln was on board.

Ironically, in some ways the advent of the Civil War facilitated the launching of the Pacific Railroad. Previously, a large stumbling block to consensus in Congress had been choosing a route. Southern representatives wanted the Pacific Railroad to run in the south, starting in New Orleans, through southern Texas, and onward through the territories of New Mexico and Arizona. Northern interests, on the other hand, wanted Chicago or St. Louis or Minneapolis as the eastern terminus. After the secession of the Confederate states, the debate in Congress on the concept of the Pacific Railroad was no longer hindered by questions about terrain, because the Southern representatives were absent.

During the autumn of 1861, Durant and others from the East lobbied aggressively. So, too, did a combination of wealthy

California businessmen—Leland Stanford, Collis P. Huntington, Charles Crocker, and Mark Hopkins—who, inspired and encouraged by engineer Theodore Judah (Dodge's functional equivalent in California), stood prepared to begin construction from Sacramento. However, it was not until January 21, 1862, that the topic of the Pacific Railroad came up on the floor, in a speech by California representative Aaron A. Sargent, who pushed it as a necessity of war. Sargent said that by building a transcontinental railroad, the federal government would save millions of dollars in transporting soldiers, artillery, and mail. He also noted that the process of construction would help quell the threat to settlers from Indians on the plains. Sargent also reminded his fellow congressmen that once the Pacific Railroad was complete, trade with Japan and China would increase, while at the same time California's loyalty to the Union would be cemented.

Sargent's eloquence led to the creation of a special committee to consider drafting a bill. Not leaving anything to chance, Theodore Judah got himself appointed clerk of the House Committee and as secretary to the Senate Pacific Railroad Committee—ideal positions for a lobbyist bent on pushing through funding for the project. As Stephen Ambrose notes,

> Fortunately for Judah, for the central Pacific, and for the line running west from the Missouri River, whatever it was to be named, the President took as active an interest as time allowed. Lincoln made it clear to the congressmen that despite the war he advocated the bill's passage and the construction of the road, and he wanted it started right away. Grenville Dodge, then serving as a general in the Union Army, said that Lincoln told him and others that the road had to be built "not only as a military necessity, but as a means of holding the Pacific Coast to the Union."

The Pacific Railway Act of 1862 was passed by the Senate on June 20, 1862—after which the House of Representatives

Grenville Mellen Dodge, who served as a brigadier general in the Union Army during the Civil War, was the Union Pacific Railroad's chief engineer from 1866 to 1870. It was Dodge who suggested that a railroad to the Pacific coast should run along the 42nd parallel, with Omaha, Nebraska, as the starting point.

promptly concurred. President Lincoln signed the final bill into law on July 1. "The Pacific Railroad is a fixed fact and you can govern yourself accordingly," Judah wrote to the editors of the *Sacramento Union*. The bill created a corporate entity called the Union Pacific, which would build west from the Missouri River, while the Central Pacific (which already existed as a corporate entity) was chartered to build east from Sacramento.

Congress capitalized the new Union Pacific at 100,000 shares selling for $1,000 each, equaling a total capitalization of $100 million. Both roads were financed with government bonds at the rate of $16,000 per mile of flat track laid, $32,000 per mile of track laid in foothills, and $48,000 per mile accomplished in mountainous terrain. The bonds were a loan—in essence, a loan of the federal government's good credit. It would be up to the railroads to sell the bonds and raise the capital with which to finance their work. The faster a company progressed, the more financing it would receive. In addition, each firm was to receive significant rights of way and land associated with each mile of track laid—not to mention revenues from those track miles for perpetuity. Thus, Lincoln and Congress very consciously set up a competitive relationship between the Union Pacific and the Central Pacific, poising them to race to a meeting point along the 42nd parallel and accomplish their work as quickly as possible.

Once the bill was passed, 44 members of the House, 17 members of the Senate, and the secretary of state presented Theodore Judah with a formal affidavit of appreciation:

> Learning of your anticipated speedy departure for California on Pacific Railroad business, we cannot let this opportunity pass without tendering to you our warmest thanks for your valuable assistance in aiding the passage of the Pacific Railroad bill through Congress. Your explorations and surveys in the Sierra Nevada Mountains have settled the question

(continues on page 22)

THEODORE JUDAH
(1826–1863)

Conceptualizing the First Transcontinental Railroad

Although he died before the completion of the Transcontinental Railroad in 1869, Theodore Judah helped lay the groundwork for its construction. Judah was unflagging in his dedication: He not only lobbied Congress, which resulted in the passage of the 1862 Pacific Railway Act, but also surveyed the route that would be used to cross California's Sierra Nevada.

Although he did not live to see his dream completed, it can be said that no man deserves the title "Father of the Transcontinental Railroad" more than Theodore Judah. Born in 1826 in Bridgeport, Connecticut, Judah was a self-taught engineer and surveyor who early on envisioned the dream of a railroad linking the Atlantic and Pacific coasts.

As a young man, Judah served as chief building engineer for the Niagara Gorge Railroad in New York State. Then, during the early 1850s, he was recruited to California to do survey work for the Sacramento Valley Railroad, a move that triggered young Judah's fascination with the idea of a transcontinental railway.

Sporadically, thereafter, he lobbied for the financing of just such a project. But his vision truly coalesced in 1860, after Daniel Strong—an early settler and entrepreneur at Dutch Flat in the Sierra Nevada foothills—showed him the best passage, via Dutch Flat,

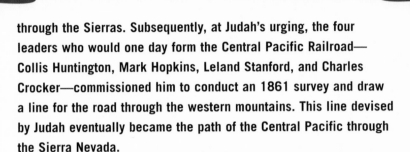

through the Sierras. Subsequently, at Judah's urging, the four leaders who would one day form the Central Pacific Railroad—Collis Huntington, Mark Hopkins, Leland Stanford, and Charles Crocker—commissioned him to conduct an 1861 survey and draw a line for the road through the western mountains. This line devised by Judah eventually became the path of the Central Pacific through the Sierra Nevada.

During 1863, Theodore Judah came down with yellow fever while crossing the Isthmus of Panama en route to New York City. He died shortly thereafter in Manhattan, with his dream unrealized.

"The project for construction of a great Railroad through the United States of America, connecting the Atlantic with the Pacific Ocean, has been in agitation for over fifteen years," Judah wrote in 1857. He continued:

> It is the most magnificent project ever conceived. It is an enterprise more important in its bearings and results to the people of the United States, than any other project involving an expenditure of an equal amount of capital. It connects these two great oceans. It is an indissoluble bond of union between the populous States of the East, and the undeveloped regions of the fruitful West. It is a highway which leads to peace and future prosperity.

"Judah," commented Collis Huntington many years after the engineer's death, "was a man of vision and a man of action. His was a dream that we made ours, and from which we profited. I have often thought, through the years, of the pity that he did not live to ride the rails—*his rails*—from Ogden to Sacramento, that he did not see the great project accomplished, and sublime history made."

(continued from page 18)

of practicalability [sic] of the line, and enabled many members to vote confidently on the great measure, while your
indefatigable exertions and intelligent explanations of the
practical features of the enterprise have gone very far to aid in
its inauguration.

The first chapter of the Pacific Railroad was thus finished.
There would be many chapters to come, all of them filled with
great accomplishment, but also with great avarice, great ambition, and great effort. Abraham Lincoln would not live to see
the bold experiment accomplished. Many others would die in
the process of the construction. Engineers would innovate and
surveyors would explore. Thousands of workers would give
their all for the greatest and most massive technological effort
yet attempted on any continent. The result would be by turns
profound but ridiculous, efficient but wasteful. But always,
from its inception to its completion and beyond, the Pacific
Railroad would be both significant and sublime.

The Race to the
Middle Begins

During the debate in Congress concerning the Pacific Railroad Bill, Representative William Holman of Indiana made the point that the railroad could never "be constructed on terms applicable to ordinary roads. . . . It is to be constructed through almost impassable mountains, deep ravines, canyons, gorges, and over arid and sandy plains. The government must come forward with a liberal hand, or the enterprise must be abandoned forever." The generous terms by which the government proposed to finance the construction attracted a fair number of charlatans intermingled with substantial and reliable businessmen.

The board and executives of the Central Pacific had already been established, but the Union Pacific was still in the process of organizing. The Pacific Railway Act mandated 163 appointed commissioners who were to define an organizational plan for the company. Most of these were political hacks: friends, supporters, and relatives of various congressmen. At the first three-day meeting held in Chicago in September 1862, only 67 of the 163 bothered to show up. They elected Samuel R. Curtis—a major general in the Union Army—chairman. They made Mayor William B. Ogden of Chicago president. And they appointed Henry V. Poor—a New Yorker and editor of the *American Railway Journal*—secretary. (Thomas Durant eventually signed on as vice president, taking responsibility for day-to-day management.)

Curtis's first order of business, he announced, would be to see to an increase in the already substantial support being offered by the government in Washington. "Notwithstanding the grant is liberal, it may still be insufficient," he said. He believed the hardest work ahead might be in the halls of Congress rather than on the western frontier. A few days later, when subscription books were opened in major cities offering Union Pacific shares, there were few takers.

DANCING WITH A WHIRLWIND

The men of the Central Pacific knew that their starting point would be Sacramento. But the eastern terminus of the Union Pacific was up for debate—though legislation stipulated that Abraham Lincoln, as president, would cast the deciding vote on this subject. During the spring of 1863, General Dodge found himself ordered to report to Lincoln for a consultation. Lincoln showed Dodge petitions from a range of towns on both sides of the Missouri River—50 miles above and below Council Bluffs— from any of which the Platte Valley route, flat for 600 miles to the start of the Rocky Mountains, could easily be embarked upon. Dodge remained emphatic that Omaha made the most sense for a starting point, and Lincoln eventually agreed. Dodge used the same meeting as an opportunity to lobby Lincoln on the deficiencies of the 1862 Pacific Railway Act with regard to funding—something the president said he would look into.

On January 8, 1863, the Central Pacific Railroad broke ground in Sacramento, California, officially marking the beginning of the construction of what would become the Transcontinental Railroad. Campsites such as the one pictured here were set up along the rail line to house Chinese workers during construction.

The Central Pacific had ceremonially broken ground for its construction project in Sacramento on January 8, 1863. The leadership of the Union Pacific was anxious to do the same as soon as possible, lest they look foolish compared to the Central Pacific and lest the Central Pacific get too large a head start on their side of the project. But Lincoln did not finally and formally put pen to paper identifying "so much of the western boundary of the State of Iowa as lies between the north and south boundaries of . . .

the city of Omaha" as the eastern terminus until November 17, 1863. Two weeks later, on December 1, the Union Pacific launched its construction with great fanfare, breaking ground in a ceremony orchestrated by chief engineer Peter Dey. However, the Union Pacific did not lay a single rail until July 1865.

Why the delay? First, even though outwardly committed to the Omaha terminus by writ of presidential decree, Vice President Durant nevertheless spent several months after the formal groundbreaking negotiating with the business leaders of adjacent communities, seeing which would offer the Union Pacific "the best deal" to make its hub in their precinct. All of this enraged Chief Engineer Dey, who found himself ordered to do a range of seemingly superfluous surveys, all meant to facilitate Durant's discussions with the various townships, one of them being the town of De Soto, 20 miles north of Omaha. Eventually, Dey complained to Dodge—still in the Union Army, but holding vast influence over the Union Pacific and its most forceful ally, Lincoln. Dey stated: "Durant is vacillating and changeable and to my mind utterly unfit to head such an enterprise. . . . It is like dancing with a whirlwind to have anything to do with him. Today matters run smoothly and tomorrow they don't." Dodge wrote Durant, "Let me advise you to drop the De Soto idea. It is one of the worst." Nevertheless, Durant continued to flirt with the leading citizens of De Soto, Florence, and Bellevue, as well as Omaha.

Secondly, there was the matter of quibbles on the part of executives from both the Central Pacific and the Union Pacific regarding funding as defined by the 1862 act. As Iowa representative Hiram Price put it, "I do not believe that there is one man in five hundred who will invest his money, and engage in the building of this road, as the law now stands."

THE PACIFIC RAILWAY ACT OF 1864

President Lincoln, the Senate, and Congress were all an easy "sell" on a revised railroad bill. As one congressman recalled: "Lincoln said to us that his experience in the West was that every railroad that had been undertaken there had broken down before it was half completed. . . . He had but one advice to us and that was to ask sufficient aid. . . . He said further that he would hurry it up so that when he retired from the presidency he could take a trip over it, it would be the proudest thing of his life that he had signed the bill in aid of its construction."

Both the Central Pacific's Collis P. Huntington and the Union Pacific's Thomas C. Durant hired lobbyists to aggressively work senators and congressmen over in support of the new railroad bill—spreading railroad bonds and other forms of government spending around liberally. In the end, the Pacific Railway Act of 1864, signed into law by Lincoln on July 2, made both the Central Pacific and the Union Pacific much more viable investment vehicles for private enterprise than they had been before.

As Stephen Ambrose has written, the act "allowed the directors of the Union Pacific and the Central Pacific to issue their own first-mortgage bonds in an amount equal to the government bonds, thus putting the government bonds in the status of a second mortgage. The government bonds [actually, the loan to the railroads] would be handed over by Washington upon the completion of twenty miles of track rather than forty. In mountainous regions the companies could collect two-thirds of their subsidy once the roadbed of a 20-mile section was prepared—that is, graded. Also, the companies were given rights, previously denied, to coal and iron and other minerals in their land grants, which were meanwhile doubled to provide ten alternate sections on each side of every mile, or about 12,800 acres per mile." Furthermore, to better attract investors, the par value of Union Pacific stock was reduced from $1,000 to $100 and additional shares issued proportionally. Additionally, the act set overlapping limits west and east for each railroad to build out, while at the same time stipulating no firm point of joining. As Union Pacific historian Maury Klein has written: "The object was to induce private parties to build the road that everyone agreed must be built."

The bill of 1864 was better than that of 1862. However, it was also flawed in that it provided vast loopholes and opportunities for fraud—opportunities that would not go unnoticed or unexploited.

CONSTRUCTION BEGINS IN EARNEST

The first phase of the project from each end—east and west—had been to survey and chart a precise path for the work, taking into account natural obstacles found in the landscape and deciding upon the most cost-efficient and negotiable routes. After the surveyors came the graders, the men who created the railroad embankment across the countryside upon which the tracks would eventually be put down.

The Union Pacific hired several hundred such workers—the lion's share of them Irish immigrants, with a few eastern Europeans mixed in, all of them recruited from such cities as Baltimore, New York, and Boston, where jobs were scarce and where anti-Irish sentiment was high. The pay of $2 to $3 a day was promised to the men, during a time when many workers only made $1 a day. The increased salary was necessary in order to induce the workers of the East to leave the cities in favor of the harsh western landscape, where amusements were few and the threats of attack by American Indians or bandits always very real. Meanwhile, the Central Pacific hired Chinese workers for most of the heavy labor of grading and track-laying. The Chinese workers were paid much less than their Irish counterparts—sometimes as little as 50¢ per day. The only difference between the Irish and the Chinese was the color of their skin, but such differences meant much in the 1860s.

As Stephen Ambrose wrote,

> The men worked with shovels, picks, wheelbarrows, teams, and scrapers. The younger men were usually the drivers, the older ones did the plowing and filling. The men in their late

During the survey stage of the Transcontinental project, engineers had to figure out the most cost-efficient and negotiable routes through natural hazards. Pictured here is the east end of the tunnel through Utah's Weber Canyon, which the Union Pacific passed through on its way to meet the Central Pacific.

teenage years or early twenties were generally the shovelers. The job of all was to lay out a grade for the track, one that was level with only a bit of curve two feet or more above the ground, so it would not be flooded out. Mainly that required digging dirt, filling a wheelbarrow with it, taking it to the grade, and dumping it. Sometimes two men used a dump wagon drawn by a horse.

Grading occupied the entire year of 1864 and much of 1865. During mid-October 1865, a reporter for the *Omaha Weekly Herald* who traveled with advance Union Pacific construction teams wrote that graders for the Union Pacific had gotten as far as Nebraska's Loup River, and that plans were being drawn for the foundations of a railroad bridge at Loup Fork. Meanwhile, trestles for the bridge were hastily being crafted in Chicago for shipment to the bridge site. As this suggests, logistics and timing were key to the efficient advancement of the railroad. While foundations were crafted for bridges to forge rivers and gorges in the middle of the country, trestles were designed and built in Chicago and Sacramento. While grades were defined and created across the stark prairies and mountains of the West, surveyors and cartographers pushed forward, delineating the further extensions of those grades.

VIRGIN LANDSCAPE

The terrain these mapmakers and graders traversed was wilderness, but they would lay the groundwork for the onslaught of development that would follow the railroad in the coming decades. James Maxwell, a young engineer working in the Platte River Valley, near the start of the westward push of the Union Pacific, came away stunned by the beauty of the tallgrass prairie, which he described as a plush "grass country. On the river bottoms it grew to be over 7 feet in height. In riding a buggy, a person would have to stand up to see over the top of the grass. In running a line through such grass, he was liable to be lost." In the same memoir, Maxwell recalled it as being "very beautiful to see the fires at night, from the various camps, circling around the hills among the short grass, but when the grass in the bottom lands caught fire, it was a grand and appalling sight." The valley was among the most fertile terrains in the country and would soon, on the heels of the railroad, be awash in settlers.

Engineers and workers for the Central Pacific encountered a wholly different geographical landscape. Instead of easy, grassy prairie and the occasional river to bridge, the Central Pacific personnel faced a harsh mountain environment. In his 1866 memoir, *Mountaineering in the Sierra Nevada*, California Geographical Survey veteran Clarence King wrote: "For four hundred miles the Sierras are a definite ridge, broad and high, and having the form of a sea-wave." Their eastern face featured "buttresses of somber-hued rock" jutting "at intervals from a steep wall." Their western face featured "long ridges of comparatively gentle outline." But, King added, "This sloping table is scored from summit to base by a system of parallel transverse canyons, distant from one another often less than twenty-five miles. They are ordinarily two or three thousand feet deep, falling at times in sheer, smooth-fronted cliffs, again in sweeping curves like the hull of a ship, with irregular, hilly flanks opening at last through gateways of low, rounded foot-hills out upon the horizontal plain of the San Joaquin and Sacramento. Every canyon carries a river, derived from the constant melting of the perpetual snow." Summits, most of them covered by glaciers, went from a mere 6,000 feet in the north to more than 14,000 feet in the south of the range.

In short, no locomotive made would be able to surmount the high peaks of the Sierra Nevada. Thus, it was necessary that tunnels—these tracing their courses through solid granite, a feat which had never been accomplished before—be created one after the other to accommodate the Central Pacific's passage through the mountains. While the engineers and laborers of the Union Pacific pushed their project through the beautiful flatlands of the tall-grass prairie, their counterparts with the Central Pacific contemplated the making of engineering history.

AROUND THE WORLD IN 80 DAYS

Thanks in part to three technological innovations that took place in 1869 to 1870—the opening of the Suez Canal in Egypt, the completion of a railroad system in India that linked the subcontinent, and the completion of the Transcontinental Railroad—French author Jules Verne found the inspiration to write his 1873 novel, *Around the World in 80 Days*. In the book, Verne's characters Phileas Fogg, a wealthy resident of London, and his French valet, Passepartout, enjoy a ride on the new Transcontinental Railroad as part of their journey around the world:

> The Central Pacific, taking Sacramento for its starting-point, extends eastward to meet the road from Omaha. . . .
>
> The train, on leaving Sacramento, and passing the junction, Rocklin, Auburn, and Colfax, entered the range of the Sierra Nevada. 'Cisco was reached at seven in the morning. . . . The railway track wound in and out among the passes, now approaching the mountain-sides, now suspended over precipices, avoiding abrupt angles by bold curves, plunging into narrow defiles, which seemed to have no outlet. The locomotive, its great funnel emitting a weird light, with its sharp bell, and its cow-catcher extended like a spur, mingled its shrieks and bellowings with the noise of torrents and cascades, and twined its smoke among the branches of the gigantic pines.
>
> The train entered the State of Nevada through the Carson Valley about nine o'clock, going always northeasterly; and at midday reached Reno. . . .
>
> From this point the road, running along Humboldt River, passed northward for several miles by its banks; then it turned eastward, and kept by the river until it reached the Humboldt Range, nearly at the extreme eastern limit of Nevada.

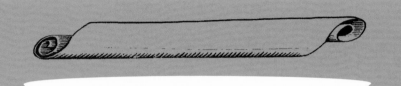

Mr. Fogg and his companions . . . observed the varied landscape which unfolded itself as they passed along the vast prairies, the mountains lining the horizon, and the creeks, with their frothy, foaming streams. Sometimes a great herd of buffaloes, massing together in the distance, seemed like a moveable dam. These innumerable multitudes of ruminating beasts often form an insurmountable obstacle to the passage of the trains; thousands of them have been seen passing over the track for hours together, in compact ranks. The locomotive is then forced to stop.

This happened, indeed, to the train in which Mr. Fogg was traveling. About twelve o'clock a troop of ten or twelve thousand head of buffalo encumbered the track. The locomotive, slackening its speed, tried to clear the way with its cow-catcher; but the mass of animals was too great. . . .

The engineer did not try to overcome the obstacle, and he was wise. He would have crushed the first buffaloes, no doubt, with the cow-catcher; but the locomotive, however powerful, would soon have been checked, the train would inevitably have been thrown off the track, and would then have been helpless.

The best course was to wait patiently, and regain the lost time by greater speed when the obstacle was removed. The procession of buffaloes lasted three full hours, and it was night before the track was clear. The last ranks of the herd were now passing over the rails, while the first had already disappeared below the southern horizon.

It was eight o'clock when the train passed through the defiles of the Humboldt Range, and half-past nine when it penetrated Utah.

The Men Who Made the Railroad

The two largest constituencies of laborers for the Central Pacific and the Union Pacific were of Chinese and Irish descent. The Chinese predominated in the work of the Central Pacific, and the Irish predominated in the work of the Union Pacific. Additionally, both firms also used some black laborers, most of whom were recently freed slaves in the employ of the Union Pacific. Each of these worker groups had their own unique story.

THE CHINESE

Some 60,000 Chinese lived in California during the 1860s, mostly around San Francisco. Like many settlers, the Chinese had first come to California in search of a new start—in search of riches—at the time of the gold rush in the late 1840s. In time, stiff and brutal racial laws kept the Chinese in the lowest of jobs, often being compensated at rates as low as $6 per month for 12-hour work days.

An 1868 article in *Lippincott's Monthly Magazine* discussed "The Chinese of California." The reporter wrote that the purpose of every worker coming to California was "to amass such a sum—trifling in our eyes—in three or four years, as in China will give him support for life." The writer praised the unceasing activity and ambition of the Chinese, and their willingness to work tirelessly for employers. "[The Chinese laborer] may have less muscle, but by his untiring persistence he accomplishes more work than the Caucasian." The writer also noted that the Chinese—unlike many white men who put themselves on the market as unskilled laborers—were smart. "[They] quickly get the 'hang' of whatever you set them at, and soon display a remarkable adroitness. . . . Every [one] reads and writes, and in figures he is our superior."

The Chinese had industriously performed the basest of tasks associated with California's first big boom, the frantic search for gold known as the gold rush of the late 1840s and early 1850s. While it was white men who reaped the greatest benefit from gold mines drilled down deep into the sides of California's mountains, it was frequently the Chinese who did the dangerous work of carving and blasting out those mines for pennies a day. Most received a hefty raise when they started working for the Central Pacific at a rate of about $31 per month on average. Their white managers called them "Celestials," in a reflection of their spiritual beliefs.

During the autumn of 1865, Central Pacific president Leland Stanford wrote a report to U.S. president Andrew Johnson concerning the use of Chinese laborers:

> A large majority of the white laboring class on the Pacific Coast find more profitable and congenial employment in mining and agricultural pursuits, than in railroad work. The greater portion of the laborers employed by us are Chinese,

Chinese workers first came to California during the gold rush of 1848–1849, when they joined tens of thousands of prospectors from the United States and abroad in the search for gold. The Chinese quickly gained a reputation as being industrious workers, which led Central Pacific officials to hire them to meet their massive manpower needs. Pictured here are Chinese workers at the Secrettown Trestle in the Sierra Nevada.

who constitute a large element in the population of California. Without them it would be impossible to complete the western portion of this great national enterprise within the time required by the Acts of Congress.

As a class they are quiet, peaceable, patient, industrious and economical—ready and apt to learn all the different kinds of work required in railroad building, they soon become as efficient as white laborers. More prudent and economical, they are contented with less wages. We find them organized into societies for mutual aid and assistance. These societies, that count their numbers by thousands, are conducted by shrewd, intelligent business men, who promptly advise their subordinates where employment can be found on the most favorable terms.

No system similar to slavery, serfdom or peonage prevails among these laborers. Their wages, which are always paid in coin, at the end of each month, are divided among them by their agents, who attend to their business, in proportion to the labor done by each person. These agents are generally American or Chinese merchants, who furnish them their supplies of food, the value of which they deduct from their monthly pay. We have assurances from leading Chinese merchants, that under the just and liberal policy pursued by the Company, it will be able to procure during the next year, not less than 15,000 laborers. With this large force, the Company will be able to push on the work so as not only to complete it far within the time required by the Acts of Congress, but so as to meet the public impatience.

The Central Pacific never amassed 15,000 laborers. As reporter Albert D. Richardson wrote in 1867, chronicling the advance of the railroad: "The cars now [1867] run nearly to the summit of the Sierras. . . . Four thousand laborers were at work—one-tenth Irish, the rest Chinese. They were a great army laying siege to Nature in her strongest citadel. The rugged mountains looked like stupendous ant-hills. . . . Irish laborers received thirty dollars per month [gold] and board; Chinese, thirty-one dollars, boarding themselves. After a little experience the latter were quite as efficient and far less troublesome."

Another reporter, writing in 1868, commented: "Systematic workers these Chinese—competent and wonderfully effective because tireless and unremitting in their industry. Order and industry then, as now, made for accomplishment. Divided into gangs of about 30 men each, they work under the direction of an American foreman. The Chinese board themselves. One of their number is selected in each gang to receive all wages and buy all provisions. They usually pay an American clerk—$1 a month apiece is usual—to see that each gets all he earned and is charged no more than his share of the living expenses. They are paid from $30 to $35 in gold a month, out of which they board themselves. They are credited with having saved about $20 a month. Their workday is from sunrise to sunset, six days in the week. They spend Sunday washing and mending, gambling and smoking, and frequently, old timers will testify, in shrill-toned quarreling."

Writing in 1865, Central Pacific chief engineer Samuel Montague reported to his superiors: "It became apparent early in the season, that the amount of labor likely to be required during the summer could only be supplied by the employment of the Chinese element, of our population. Some distrust was at first felt regarding the capacity of this class for the service required, but the experiment has proved eminently successful. They are faithful and industrious, and under proper supervision, soon become skillful in the performance of their duties. Many of them are becoming very expert in drilling, blasting, and other departments of rock work."

At the very start of the Transcontinental project, James Harvey Strobridge—superintendent of the Central Pacific and a native of Ireland—refused to hire Chinese workers based purely on prejudice. But when white laborers proved hard to retain, Central Pacific investor Charles Crocker insisted that Strobridge give the Chinese a try. "They built the Great Wall of China, didn't they?" Crocker is reported to have said in the midst of an argument with Strobridge. "Who says laborers have to be white to build railroads?" After about a month of supervising the Chinese, Strobridge had to admit that they were superb all around. The men worked well together, learned quickly, and performed their tasks swiftly but safely. Their one indiscretion and diversion was opium, a drug that many smoked on Sunday, their day off, while their white counterparts attended religious services. During the spring of 1869, after the last spike on the Transcontinental Railroad had been driven into the ground, according to published reports, Strobridge "invited [several] Chinese . . . to dine at his boarding car. When they entered, all the guests and officers present cheered them as the chosen representatives of the race which have greatly helped to build the road . . . a tribute they well deserved and which evidently gave them much pleasure."

The Chinese—like their Irish counterparts—spent summers in large tents pitched along the grade of the railroad. During the winters, they lived in wooden bunkhouses beside the track, and were transported to their workplace by trains that carried them to the end of the line. Overall, the Chinese ate better than their white counterparts. While the Irish workers lived almost entirely on boiled beef and potatoes, the Chinese ate a more varied diet. They kept themselves well supplied with vegetables. They also brought live pigs and chickens along with them for fresh meat. Also, while the Irish restricted their nonalcoholic liquid intake to water, often derived from the same streams where the work crews relieved themselves, the Chinese routinely drank tea. Through boiling water in the making of the tea, the Chinese thus avoided the intestinal disease called dysentery, which plagued the white workers.

While the relatively easy and skilled work of building trestles, laying rails, and masonry was reserved for whites, who were paid more, the Chinese were routinely handed the intensive and more dangerous chores of shoveling grades, felling trees, and drilling holes for black powder used to blast tunnels.

"I can assure you," wrote one foreman addressing a letter to a California State representative in Congress, "the Chinese are moving the earth and rock rapidly. They prove nearly equal to

CHARLES NORDHOFF
(1830–1901)

Telling the Story
of the Transcontinental Railroad

Writing four years after the completion of the Transcontinental Railroad, in his book *California for Health, Pleasure, and Residence: A Book for Travellers and Settlers* (1873), popular author Charles Nordhoff painted the background of the genesis of the Central Pacific Railroad and the various debates that loomed about the commencement of the laying of rails through the Sierra Nevada. Nordhoff did a good job of describing the seeming impossibility of the project as viewed by many. He also did a good job of explaining the many logistical hurdles attendant to the building of the railroad—ones surmounted only through sheer force of will on the part of the workers challenged with the task.

Five Sacramento merchants, who undertook to build a railroad through eight hundred miles of an almost uninhabited country, over mountains and across an alkali desert, were totally unknown to the great money world; that their project was pronounced impracticable by engineers of reputation testifying before legislative committees; that it was opposed and ridiculed at every step by the moneyed men of San Francisco; that even in their own neighborhood they were thought sure to fail; and the "Dutch Flat Swindle," as their project was called, was caricatured, written down in pamphlets, abused in newspapers, spoken against by politicians, denounced by capitalists, and for a long time held in such ill repute that it was more than a

white men in the amount of labor they perform, and are more reliable. No danger of strikes among them ... I tell you ... we are in dead earnest about the R.R."

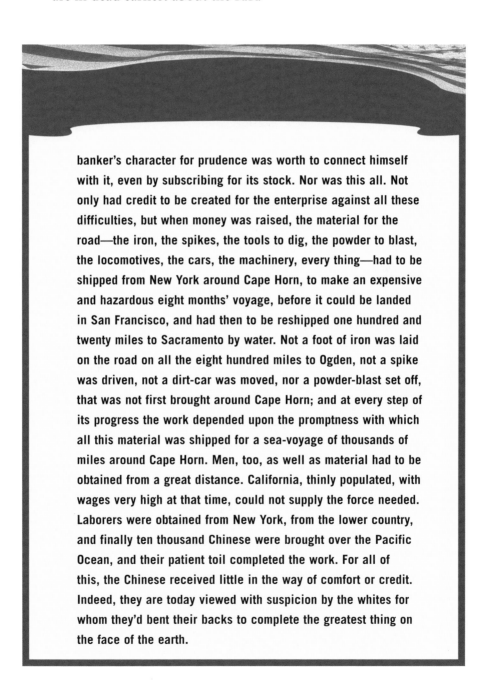

banker's character for prudence was worth to connect himself with it, even by subscribing for its stock. Nor was this all. Not only had credit to be created for the enterprise against all these difficulties, but when money was raised, the material for the road—the iron, the spikes, the tools to dig, the powder to blast, the locomotives, the cars, the machinery, every thing—had to be shipped from New York around Cape Horn, to make an expensive and hazardous eight months' voyage, before it could be landed in San Francisco, and had then to be reshipped one hundred and twenty miles to Sacramento by water. Not a foot of iron was laid on the road on all the eight hundred miles to Ogden, not a spike was driven, not a dirt-car was moved, nor a powder-blast set off, that was not first brought around Cape Horn; and at every step of its progress the work depended upon the promptness with which all this material was shipped for a sea-voyage of thousands of miles around Cape Horn. Men, too, as well as material had to be obtained from a great distance. California, thinly populated, with wages very high at that time, could not supply the force needed. Laborers were obtained from New York, from the lower country, and finally ten thousand Chinese were brought over the Pacific Ocean, and their patient toil completed the work. For all of this, the Chinese received little in the way of comfort or credit. Indeed, they are today viewed with suspicion by the whites for whom they'd bent their backs to complete the greatest thing on the face of the earth.

THE IRISH

As has been noted, Irish workers were a minority in the Central Pacific project. But they were a majority in the Union Pacific project. Like the Chinese, most Irish workers were diligent and hard-working. Unlike the docile Chinese—who silently and serenely enjoyed their opium once a week—many of the Irish enjoyed their whiskey and beer every night, and were known to be loud and boisterous carousers who liked to blow off steam on a regular basis. Also unlike the Chinese, Irish workers had an air of rebellion about them. Many openly talked of unionizing and of labor strikes or slowdowns whenever pay arrived late or was less than expected. Where managers and superintendents with the Central Pacific could take their Chinese workers largely for granted, authorities with the Union Pacific had to always be attentive to the wants and needs of their workforce, lest progress on the project be slowed down. (Eventually, however, the Central Pacific's Chinese workers would briefly go on strike over wages.)

Entrepreneurs cashed in on the Irish workers' need for boisterous entertainment. Gamblers, women, and saloon keepers advanced across the countryside in step with the railroads. An entire town hauled on wagons and flatbed cars, called "Hell on Wheels," followed the men, offering makeshift taverns, gambling parlors, dance halls, and prostitutes. Transcontinental Railroad historian Carol Bowers remarks:

> End of tracks towns sprang up very quickly as the railroad came along. Many of the buildings were tents, maybe four posts in the ground with a canvas top for a cover. Many of the gambling halls and the saloons would operate 24 hours a day, and one of the things that settlers mentioned frequently in their letters and journals was the annoyance from the noise of these gambling halls and the saloons. . . . It was very noisy, very crowded and very rough. Most of the women coming along in that point were entrepreneurs. They were

Like the Chinese, Irish workers were ambitious and hard-working and were brought onboard to work on both the Union Pacific and Central Pacific railroads. Pictured here are Irish laborers working on the Central Pacific Railroad in Nevada.

prostitutes who were there primarily for the same reason that the men were following this westward press of empire, which was to make quick money and lots of it. And so they would locate themselves wherever there was a fluid population of men with money to spend.

Other camp followers of both the Union Pacific and Central Pacific included numerous priests of the Roman

Catholic Church. The advance teams of both the Union Pacific and Central Pacific also included a fair share of reporters, who invented a new, vague, and exotic location identifier for their

JAMES ABRAM KLEISER
(1818–1906)

Telling the Story of the Railroad Workers

James Abram Kleiser served as a construction engineer with the Central Pacific Railroad and was much involved with the construction of trestles crossing gorges, as well as snow sheds. His brief memoir paints a vivid—and grim—picture of some of the hazards that railroad construction workers routinely faced. What follows is an excerpt from his journal:

February, 1867, I went on the Central Pacific Railroad to build bridges on the Truckee River. I was still in debt. . . . I worked all summer at a good salary and sometime in November when I was raising a bridge at the Cascades above Cisco and had it nearly completed I accidentally made a misstep and fell from the top, a distance of fifty feet, breaking six ribs and injuring my shoulder and spine. I was unconscious until the next day and was not able to walk for nearly two months. . . . The next Spring I went back to Cisco on the Central Pacific and got up plans for a machine to frame timber for the snow-sheds. In March went down the Truckee to the State line and had a gang of men getting out ties for the railroad. In May moved the gang to Cold Stream, above Truckee, and made ties until the first of June. I then got orders to go to Sacramento and have my machine built at the Company's shops. I had my machine finished by the 20th of June and shipped it up to Summit Valley. Put in a side

reports from unmapped terrain—the "End of the Tracks"—and who enjoyed the diversions of "Hell on Wheels" just as much as the workers did.

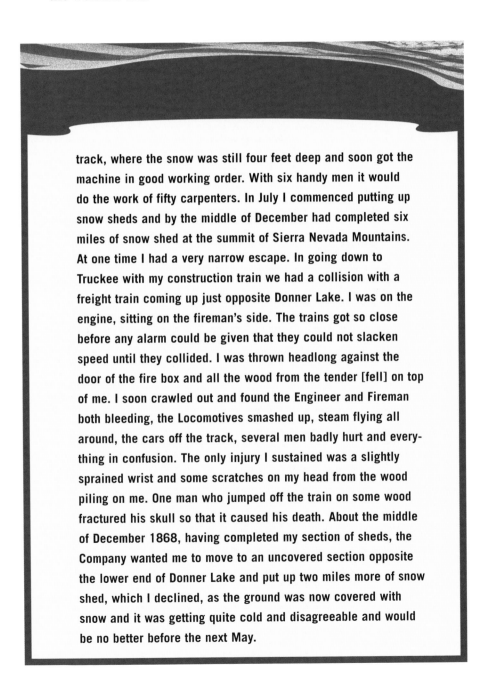

track, where the snow was still four feet deep and soon got the machine in good working order. With six handy men it would do the work of fifty carpenters. In July I commenced putting up snow sheds and by the middle of December had completed six miles of snow shed at the summit of Sierra Nevada Mountains. At one time I had a very narrow escape. In going down to Truckee with my construction train we had a collision with a freight train coming up just opposite Donner Lake. I was on the engine, sitting on the fireman's side. The trains got so close before any alarm could be given that they could not slacken speed until they collided. I was thrown headlong against the door of the fire box and all the wood from the tender [fell] on top of me. I soon crawled out and found the Engineer and Fireman both bleeding, the Locomotives smashed up, steam flying all around, the cars off the track, several men badly hurt and every-thing in confusion. The only injury I sustained was a slightly sprained wrist and some scratches on my head from the wood piling on me. One man who jumped off the train on some wood fractured his skull so that it caused his death. About the middle of December 1868, having completed my section of sheds, the Company wanted me to move to an uncovered section opposite the lower end of Donner Lake and put up two miles more of snow shed, which I declined, as the ground was now covered with snow and it was getting quite cold and disagreeable and would be no better before the next May.

THE WORK THEY DID, THE PROGRESS THEY MADE

The work of grading was grueling and intensive—bending down low to dig, shoveling for hours, tossing dirt up on high embankments, hauling ballast by the cartload—all toward building a level foundation for the track. Then, the next crews came along, picking up cut railway ties from horse-drawn wagons and carefully placing them on the grade, evenly spaced. A third crew laid the rails, foremen carefully measuring every stretch to make sure the rails were spread apart at exactly 4 feet, 8½ inches—known as "standard gauge." Then a fourth squad of workers spiked the tracks down. Each spike received three blows from a heavy sledgehammer. The last step consisted of connecting the ends of the rails with a fishplate. On the Central Pacific's project, laborers had the additional task of blasting tunnels through the mountains—a slow, tedious, and dangerous process inhibited by the limits of black powder, an explosive that was only capable of producing small blasts and caused work to progress slowly.

Thus, overall, one would have expected the Union Pacific to make much better headway on a mile-per-day calculation than the Central Pacific. But, as we shall see, this was not immediately the case.

Corruption

As has been previously noted, the Pacific Railway acts of 1862 and 1864 were meant to inspire and facilitate the construction of the two rail lines linking the Missouri River with the West Coast of the United States. In this spirit, the acts provided land grants (together with title to coal and iron found on those lands) stretching the distance of the proposed line. The bills also supplied capital in the form of subsidy bonds (representing a second mortgage) to be doled out upon the completion of each 20-mile section of track. They further authorized other private firms to develop branches feeding the Union Pacific, which would eventually develop into such lines as the Kansas Pacific, the Denver Pacific, and the Missouri Pacific. To help fund these operations, Congress authorized the Union Pacific to issue its own convertible first-mortgage bonds upon approval of its 20-member board of directors, five of whom were federal appointees.

THE CRÉDIT MOBILIER

Irregularities in financing cropped up early. Those who purchased the first-mortgage bonds and converted them to stock—among them Thomas Durant; brothers Oakes and Oliver Ames (the former a member of Congress from Massachusetts), both of whom had amassed small fortunes manufacturing picks and shovels at their factory in Easton, Massachusetts, during the gold rush; Director Sidney Dillon; and a number of other investors—tended to have hidden agendas. Of them all, Durant was the most powerful. During 1864, Durant purchased numerous Union Pacific bonds and secured himself a place on the board. Following a power struggle with the Ames brothers, during which he tried to snare the title of president, Durant wound up as vice president and general manager.

In this capacity, Durant made sure the railroad's first exorbitantly priced construction contract (at costs per mile some two to three times higher than necessary) went to one H. M. Hoxie, who was the agent for a Pennsylvania corporation that Durant, Oakes Ames, Dillon, and a few other investors had acquired a year earlier and renamed the Crédit Mobilier of America. The Crédit Mobilier in turn subcontracted the work, on equally generous terms, to firms owned or controlled by various other Union Pacific board members. Three years later, in 1867, the Crédit Mobilier awarded a new construction contract to Oakes Ames, who (like Hoxie before him) subcontracted with firms owned by board members to build still more track. Construction profits were later estimated to be between $7 million and $23 million. This process depleted generous congressional grants to the Union Pacific and left the railroad under heavy debt by the time of its completion in 1869.

In 1864, Union Pacific vice president Thomas Durant, pictured here (second from left, at the table) with fellow controlling partners of the railroad, formed the Crédit Mobilier of America company. Durant's company was the lone bidder on the construction project for the Union Pacific Railroad and was created to limit liability for its stockholders and maximize construction profits.

TANGLED WEBS

Many critics complained about the perpetual frauds of what some began to call the "Pacific Railroad Ring." As early as 1867, Oakes Ames worked in Congress to forestall federal investigations into these allegations. He did so by bribing colleagues in the House and Senate. Ames assigned large blocks of Crédit Mobilier stock to specially selected colleagues at well below market value. Speaker of the House Schuyler Colfax agreed to take shares from Crédit Mobilier, as did Massachusetts senator Henry Wilson, Ohio representative (and future president) James A. Garfield, Senator James W. Patterson of New Hampshire, and representatives Henry Laurens Dawes of Massachusetts, John Bingham of Ohio, John A. Logan of Illinois, and William B. Allison and James F. Wilson of Iowa. Ames also involved two Pennsylvania representatives: William D. "Pig-Iron" Kelly and G. W. Scofield. Like Ames, most of the participants in the Crédit Mobilier were Republicans. The scheme's lone Democrat—James Brooks of New York—served as a government-appointed director of the Union Pacific and was thus prohibited by law from owning company shares. He got around this problem by buying some stock in his son's name.

The only members to eventually get cold feet were Allison and both Wilsons. They returned their holdings in 1869. Other members of Congress, whom Ames approached, such as Maine's James G. Blaine, declined to get involved in the first place. Ames kept track of all transactions in a little black ledger book. He wrote his associate Henry S. McComb that he had placed the Crédit Mobilier stock "where it will produce the most good to us." Ames subsequently forwarded to McComb several lists of congressmen who had received or were to receive shares. Later on, in 1872, during that year's presidential election campaign, friction between Ames and McComb led to the publication of the letters in Charles A. Dana's *New York Sun*, thus sparking a scandal that led to two full congressional investigations.

THE POLAND COMMITTEE'S REPORT
ON THE CRÉDIT MOBILIER

During December 1872, the House of Representatives appointed a committee headed by Representative Luke P. Poland, a Republican from Vermont, to look into the Crédit Mobilier affair. A few months later, the Poland Committee issued its report as to the guilt of key players in the scheme. Some of the committee's findings were as follows.

With regard to Henry Laurens Dawes, the committee noted:

Mr. Dawes had, prior to December, 1867, made some small investments in railroad bonds through Mr. Ames. In December 1867, Mr. Dawes applied to Mr. Ames to purchase a $1,000 bond of the Cedar Rapids Road, in Iowa. Mr. Ames informed him that he had sold them all, but that he would let him have for his $1,000 ten shares of Credit Mobilier stock, which he thought was better than the railroad bonds. In answer to inquiry by Mr. Dawes, Mr. Ames said the Credit Mobilier Company had the contract to build the Union Pacific Road, and thought they would make money out of it, and that it would be a good thing; that he would guarantee that he should get ten per cent on his money, and that if at any time Mr. Dawes did not want the stock, he would pay back his money, with ten per cent interest. Mr. Dawes made some further inquiry in relation to the stock of Mr. John B. Alley, who said he thought it was good stock, but not as good as Mr. Ames thought; but that Mr. Ames's guarantee would make it a perfectly safe investment. Mr. Dawes thereupon concluded to purchase the ten shares, and on the 11th of January he paid Mr. Ames $800, and in a few days thereafter the balance of the price of the stock at par, and interest from the July previous. In June, 1868, Mr. Ames received a dividend of sixty per cent in money on his stock, and of it paid to Mr. Dawes $400, and applied the balance of $200 upon accounts between them. This $400 was all that was paid

Along with Thomas Durant, Massachusetts congressman Oakes Ames helped establish Crédit Mobilier of America in 1864. However, it was Ames who took the brunt of the punishment after a congressional investigation discovered that he had been selling company stock to his fellow congressmen at a discounted rate.

over to Mr. Dawes as a dividend upon this stock. At some time prior to December 1868, Mr. Dawes was informed that a suit had been commenced in the courts of Pennsylvania by the former owners of the charter of the Credit Mobilier, claiming that those then claiming and using it had no right to do so. Mr. Dawes thereupon informed Mr. Ames that as there was a litigation about the matter, he did not desire to keep the stock. On the 9th of December, 1868, Mr. Ames and Mr. Dawes had a settlement of these matters, in which Mr. Dawes was allowed for the money he paid for the stock, with ten per cent interest upon it, and accounted to Mr. Ames for the $400 he had received as a dividend. Mr. Dawes received no other benefit under the contract than to get ten per cent upon his money, and after the settlement had no further interest in the stock.

With regard to G. W. Scofield:

In 1866, Mr. Scofield purchased some Cedar Rapids bonds of Mr. Ames, and in that year they had conversation about Mr. Scofield taking stock in the Credit Mobilier Company, but no contract was consummated. In December, 1867, Mr. Scofield applied to Mr. Ames to purchase more Cedar Rapids bonds, when Mr. Ames suggested that he should purchase some Credit Mobilier stock, and explained generally that it was a contracting company to build the Union Pacific Road; that, as it was a Pennsylvania corporation, he would like to have some Pennsylvanian in it; that he would sell it to him at par and interest, and that he would guarantee he should get eight per cent if Mr. Scofield would give him half the dividends above that. Mr. Scofield said he thought he would take $1,000 of the stock, but before anything further was done Mr. Scofield was called home by sickness in his family. On his return, in the latter part of January 1868, he spoke to Mr. Ames about the stock, when Mr. Ames said he thought it was all sold, but he would take his money and give him a receipt and get the stock for him if he could. Mr. Scofield therefore paid Mr. Ames $1041, and took his receipt therefore. Not long after Mr. Ames informed Mr. Scofield he could have the stock, but could not give him a certificate for it until he could get a larger certificate dividend. Mr. Scofield received the bond dividend of eighty per cent, which was payable January 3, 1868, taking a bond for $1,000, and paying Mr. Ames the difference. Mr. Ames received the sixty per cent cash dividend on the stock in June, 1868, and paid over to Mr. Scofield $600, the amount of it. Before the close of that session of Congress, which was toward the end of July, Mr. Scofield became, for some reason, disinclined to take the stock, and a settlement was made between them, by which Mr. Ames was to retain the Credit Mobilier stock and Mr. Scofield took $1,000 Union Pacific stock. The precise basis of the settlement does not appear, neither Mr. Ames nor Mr. Scofield having any full data in reference to it. Mr. Scofield thinks that he only received back his money and interest upon it. While Mr. Ames states that he thinks Mr. Scofield had ten shares of Union Pacific stock in addition. The Committee does not deem it specially important to settle this difference of recollection. Since that settlement Mr. Scofield has had no interest in the Credit Mobilier stock, and derived no benefit there from.

With regard to James Garfield:

The facts in regard to Mr. Garfield, as found by the Committee, are identical with the case of Mr. Kelley to the point of reception of the check for $329. He agreed with Mr. Ames to take ten shares of Credit Mobilier stock, but did not pay for the same. Mr. Ames received the eighty per cent dividend in bonds, and sold them for ninety-seven per cent, and also received the sixty per cent cash dividend, which, together with the price of the stock and interest, left a balance of $329. This sum was paid over to Mr. Garfield by a check on the Sergeant-at-Arms. Mr. Ames received all the subsequent dividends, and the Committee does not find that since the payment of the $329 there has been any

James Garfield was among those who agreed to purchase Crédit Mobilier stock at reduced rates from Oakes Ames to block the congressional investigation into the company's corruption. Garfield, who is pictured here during his days as a major general in the U.S. Army, would go on to become the twentieth president of the United States.

communication between Mr. Ames and Mr. Garfield on the subject, until this investigation began. Some correspondence between Mr. Garfield and Mr. Ames, and some conversation between them during this investigation, will be found in the reported testimony.

And with regard to John Bingham:

In December, 1867, Mr. Ames advised Mr. Bingham to invest in the stock of the Credit Mobilier, assuring him that it would return him his money with profitable dividends. Mr. Bingham agreed to take twenty shares, and about the 1st of January, 1868, paid to Mr. Ames the par value of the stock, for which Mr. Ames executed to him one receipt or agreement. Mr. Ames received all the dividends on the stock or money. Some were delivered to Mr. Bingham, and some retained by Mr. Ames. The matter was not finally adjusted between them until February, 1872, when it was settled by Mr. Ames retaining the thirty shares of Credit Mobilier stock, and accounting to Mr. Bingham for such dividends upon it as Mr. Bingham had not already received. Mr. Bingham was treated as the real owner of the stock from the time of the agreement to take it in December, 1867, to the settlement in February, 1872, and had the benefit of all the dividends upon it. Neither Mr. Ames nor Mr. Bingham had such records of their dealing as to be able to give the precise amount of these dividends.

FINAL RESULT OF THE CRÉDIT MOBILIER

Few in Congress who were involved with the Crédit Mobilier came away unscathed by the disgrace of the scandal, although James Garfield went on to become president. Oakes Ames died a wealthy man in 1873, not long after his disgrace. Virtually all of the private sector businessmen involved with the Crédit

Mobilier scheme wound up keeping the fortunes they had made through the transactions of the Mobilier, and went on to lead lives as respected business leaders.

Thomas Durant lived until 1885, enjoying all the luxuries attendant to great wealth. An associate described him as "the most extravagant man I ever knew in my life." Oliver Ames lived until 1877, respected and revered in his home state of Massachusetts. Nevertheless, as Stephen Ambrose has written, "No greater breach of the public trust had as yet been transacted in the history of the United States. Ironically, the most monumental building and engineering project yet attempted on the face of the earth had led to the most monumental fraud ever perpetuated on a people and a nation. The first fortunes made in the Transcontinental Railroad had nothing to do with moving freight or passengers from one side of the country to the other. No, the first fortunes made had everything to do with gouging the American taxpayer exorbitant prices for beds graded, bridges built, and track laid—and then not passing one thin nickel of that grossly enlarged margin to the men who did the work of building the road. Thus did Durant and his cohorts cushion their seats?"

Union Pacific Progress

Early in the Union Pacific project, Thomas Durant had bragged that he would have the first hundred miles of track built by the end of 1865. This was either a confident boast, wishful thinking, or a combination of both. The Pacific Railway Act of 1864 required that the Union Pacific lay down a minimum of 100 miles of track by June 27, 1866—and in reality, Durant struggled to do even that.

UNION PACIFIC DELAYS AND DURESS

During September 1865, Durant admitted to friends that his forecast of laying 100 miles of track by the end of the year was erroneous. Indeed, he said, they would be lucky if 60 miles of track were laid by the end of the year. But then he didn't even come close to hitting that conservative benchmark. By December 31, 1865, the Union Pacific had laid just 40 miles. This, however, was enough to garner the railroad significant funding with which it positioned itself to continue with renewed vigor in the spring of 1866.

Under the terms of the 1864 act, every 20 miles of track laid entitled the railroads to $320,000 in bonds—$16,000 per mile. Thus, 40 miles of track entitled the Union Pacific to $640,000 in bonds. With these proceeds, Durant set about gathering at Omaha an enormous cadre of workers with which he would strike out as soon as warm weather emerged in the spring. But the media was wary. "We confess," wrote the editors of the *Railroad Record*, "that we are not satisfied. Neither is the country, which has a right to expect more vigor in its [the railroad's] construction."

That winter, Durant insisted that his surveyors make utmost progress in laying out the detail of the path for the track in the remote West, far from where Union Pacific workers would begin their labors in the spring. One Samuel Reed explored the distant region beyond the valley of the Great Salt Lake in Utah, defining a route from Salt Lake City to the Sierra Nevada. Eventually, after exploring the terrain in detail, Reed sent back good news to Durant. The surveyor said he could draw a straight line from Salt Lake to the valley of the Humboldt River "without a cut or fill exceeding 15 feet or grades exceeding 75 feet per mile." In other words it seemed, on the face of it, the Union Pacific would have clear sailing for many hundreds of miles.

REED, THE CASEMENTS, AND DODGE

In January 1866, three government commissioners from Washington came to inspect the Union Pacific's 40 miles of track prior to release of the bonds. Durant and Alvin Saunders, the governor of Nebraska Territory, accompanied the inspectors on what was—according to the *Omaha Weekly Herald*—"one of the loveliest winter mornings that ever dawned." The group traveled in a railroad car pulled by an engine named the

In January 1866, federal commissioners visited Nebraska, where the Union Pacific had recently completed the first 40 miles of track on its section of the Transcontinental Railroad. After taking a ride on the line, the commissioners wired President Andrew Johnson to authorize the release of the government bonds that financed the construction of the railroad.

General Sherman, moving at a rate of approximately 35 miles per hour, an astonishingly high speed for those times. Once the inspectors got back to Omaha, they wired Secretary of the Interior James Harlan that the 40 miles of track were indeed complete and "in superior condition." Shortly thereafter, President Andrew Johnson released the bonds.

The commissioners also took time to comment on and compliment Durant's "personal omnipresence in every department of the work, his vigilant and untiring watchfulness of all details, and the energy and effective push which he had imparted to the colossal enterprise." So wrote a reporter for the *New York Herald*.

A couple of months later, the *Herald* ran an editorial in which it praised Durant again, calling him "the Great Manager, who is to railroads what Napoleon was to war."

Early in 1866, intent on improving the progress of the Union Pacific, Durant fired his core group of managers who were not working fast enough. He recalled the ambitious Samuel Reed from surveying and put him in charge of the construction. Henceforth, it would be up to Reed to directly manage all grading, track laying, bridge building, and, when necessary, tunneling. During February, the brothers John and Dan Casement were put in place under Reed, with direct primary responsibility for track laying. Both had long personal experience laying track in Ohio, and the former had risen to the rank of brigadier general in the Union Army during the Civil War. The latter was also a veteran.

Most importantly, Durant succeeded in wooing Grenville Dodge—still a general with the Union Army—to become chief engineer of the railroad. Near the end of April 1866, Durant rendezvoused with Dodge at St. Joseph, Missouri, and lobbied the general to take the plunge. In the end, Dodge accepted the assignment—pending approval by his superior, General Sherman—on the condition that he have absolute authority. To Durant he pledged that he would "obey orders and insist on everyone under me doing the same." Shortly thereafter, Sherman—a great fan of the Transcontinental Railroad—agreed to a request for relief of duty from Dodge. "I consent to your going to begin what, I trust, will be the real beginning of the great road," wrote Sherman.

Thereafter, Dodge assembled the command structure of the Union Pacific on a military basis. "Nearly all his chief subordinates," writes Stephen Ambrose, "had been in the Union Army, and with but a few exceptions his graders and track layers had been participants in the war. There were thousands of them, with more coming. Military discipline came naturally to them, for they were accustomed to giving or receiving and carrying out orders. Without that military organization, it is doubtful that the Union Pacific could have been built at all. The Union Pacific had farther to go than the Central Pacific, and hostile Indians to contend with, plus shortages and nonexistence of timber, water, and other necessities."

THE THREATS OF INDIANS

Simultaneous with the building of the Transcontinental Railroad, the native residents of the American plains began to feel seriously threatened by the general incursion of white settlers onto their lands. The Homestead Act (1862) gave each adult settler a 160-acre parcel of land in the territories of the West—and the offer attracted thousands. Nebraska filled up with white settlers from the East so quickly that by 1867 it qualified to become a full-fledged state within the Union. Meanwhile, Native Americans saw their traditional hunting grounds despoiled and fought against government attempts to relegate them to reservations. In doing so, they took up arms and threatened both the new settlers and the workers building the Union Pacific.

Unlike other tribes of the Great Plains, by 1866, the Pawnee of Nebraska had mostly surrendered to the whites. They lived tranquilly, but were also—according to one contemporary observer—"more degraded in their habits and ways of living than almost any tribe." In the western part of the state, however, the Sioux and Cheyenne tribes attempted to hold on to their land. They posed a serious threat to settlers, and to the railroad, as they set out to defend their territory. General John Pope described the situation in a way that was sympathetic to the Native Americans: "The Indian, in truth, no longer has a country. He is reduced to starvation or to warring to the death. The Indian's first demand is that the white man shall not drive off his game and dispossess him of his lands. How can we promise this unless we prohibit emigration and settlement? . . . The end is sure and dreadful to contemplate." Other white leaders—

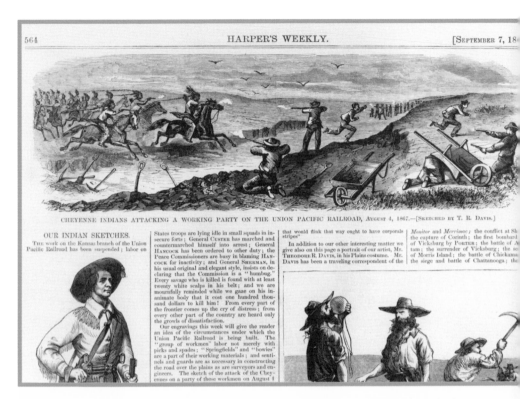

CHEYENNE INDIANS ATTACKING A WORKING PARTY ON THE UNION PACIFIC RAILROAD, AUGUST 4, 1867.—[SKETCHED BY T. R. DAVIS.]

OUR INDIAN SKETCHES.

THE work on the Kansas branch of the Union Pacific Railroad has been suspended; labor on states troops are lying idle in small squads in insecure forts; General CUSTER has marched and countermarched himself into arrest; General HANCOCK has been ordered to other duty; the Peace Commissioners are busy in blaming HANCOCK for inactivity; and General SHERMAN, in his usual original and elegant style, insists on declaring that the Commission is a "humbug." Every savage who is killed is found with at least twenty white scalps in his belt; and we are mournfully reminded while we gaze on his inanimate body that it cost one hundred thousand dollars to kill him! From every part of the frontier comes up the cry of distress; from every other part of the country are heard only the growls of dissatisfaction.

Our engravings this week will give the reader an idea of the circumstances under which the Union Pacific Railroad is being built. The "group of workmen" labor not merely with picks and spades; "Springfields" and "bowies" are a part of their working materials; and sentinels and guards are as necessary in constructing the road over the plains as are surveyors and engineers. The sketch of the attack of the Cheyennes on a party of these workmen on August 1 that would think that way ought to have corporals stripes"

In addition to our other interesting matter we give also on this page a portrait of our artist, Mr. THEODORE R. DAVIS, in his Plains costume. Mr. DAVIS has been a traveling correspondent of the

Monitor and *Merrimac*; the conflict at Sh the capture of Corinth; the first bombard of Vicksburg by PORTER; the battle of A tam; the surrender of Vicksburg; the so of Morris Island; the battle of Chickama the siege and battle of Chattanooga; the

During the construction of the Union Pacific Railroad, workers were met with fierce resistance from the Cheyenne and Sioux tribes in western Nebraska. Pictured here is an excerpt from the September 7, 1867, issue of *Harper's Weekly*, in which a party of Cheyennes is attacking a group of Union Pacific workers.

including Dodge, Durant, and General Philip Sheridan—were less charitable in their assessment. Dodge insisted that there really were "no friendly Indians."

According to Stephen Ambrose, the Sioux and Cheyennes west of Columbus, Nebraska, were "decidedly hostile. They despised the iron rail, which along with providing great benefits to the whites had an additional disadvantage for the Indians in that it split the Great Plains buffalo herd into two parts, because buffalo would not cross the tracks. The Indians wanted the iron rail, and the men who surveyed for it and the men who were building it and the farmers who were following it and the travelers who were sure to come on it, out of their country. And they had plenty of men, young and even old, who were ready to follow a war chief on a raid, against either the settlements of the surveyors or the graders or the road builders."

The army and cavalry in the region provided some measure of protection, but were understaffed. Thus, vast stretches of the sprawling railroad would always be vulnerable to attack. Recognizing this, Dodge issued instructions that every Union Pacific worker—whether surveyor or grader or rail-layer—was to be armed. They were told to always work with their rifles in easy reach. Many of the Union Pacific construction workers were veterans of the Union Army, and well trained and experienced in the ways of warfare. In short order, of necessity, they would become skilled at warding off Indian attacks.

The men building the Central Pacific, on the other hand, had little to fear from Native Americans. As John Hoyt Williams writes in the book *A Great and Shining Road: The Epic Story of the Transcontinental Railroad*,

> While the Union Pacific was led in the field by generals, protected by generals, and worked by armed veterans of every rank, the Central Pacific, spared the threat of Indian depredations, had little need of the military. The primitive Digger Indians of that part of the Sierras being pierced by [James] Strobridge's men were—through epidemics—mere memories. Descending from the Sierras to the Truckee and the flatlands below, however, the Central Pacific's surveyors encountered Indians neither primitive nor mere memories. Here lay the lands of the Paiute, Shoshone, and several migratory branches of the ferocious Apache. In 1863, by the Ruby Valley Treaty, various tribes had assented to open their lands (at least a very narrow strip of them) to be used for and by the railroads—a vaguely understood concession

to the right of eminent domain—and, for the most part, they had remained peaceful. The Central Pacific, which was granted permission by the Nevada legislature to build through the state only in 1866, was taking no chances. In that year the company signed its own treaties with the dreaded Apache subtribes, Paiutes, and others—treaties replete with generous "gifts," better defined as bribes. Some of the Indians, notably the Apaches, did not, of course, become converts to philosophical pacifism, but their warpaths seldom intersected the path of the railroad, with which they had a satisfactory arrangement. Not dependent upon the buffalo for their way of life, Nevada's Indians had less to fear from the railroad than did the Indians of the Plains. In fact, the company was to encounter only one potentially dangerous Indian problem along its entire route from Sacramento to Promontory . . . and that passed without much bloodshed.

THE 100TH MERIDIAN AND THE UNION PACIFIC

Grenville Dodge's crews got off to a late start in the spring of 1866 due to bad weather, but were eventually able to claim 100 miles of track by the deadline of the end of June. After that, however, they worked diligently and picked up speed, making great progress. Finally—on October 6—they reached a vital benchmark: the 100th meridian west (100° west longitude), now the town of Cozad, Nebraska, which is approximately 250 miles west of Omaha. More than just a line of longitude on the map, the 100th meridian represented a great symbol as the ultimate demarcation point between East and West—the line that, according to cartographers, defined the exact spot where the unirrigated, water-plentiful East ended, and the water-hungry West began. Thus, from the perspective of watersheds, the Union Pacific truly entered the West on October 6, 1866.

The 100th meridian also represented 250 miles of undisputedly complete Union Pacific track. Understanding the need to publicize progress to the public and bolster support for the project, Dodge and Durant (the latter recently elected president of the Union Pacific) made a point of turning the achievement of the 100th meridian into a media event. More than 200 celebrity guests—including titled nobles from Europe and numerous bankers and investors from Wall Street, all accompanied by a host of reporters—rode in a luxury train from New York City (departing October 15) to Chicago, and thence to the 100th meridian.

Eventually, as historian William Brey writes, the special train "finally reached a point 30 miles *beyond* the hundredth Meridian . . . where . . . a large and brilliantly illuminated encampment awaited them. End-of-track was still nowhere in sight as rails were then being laid at a rate of nearly two miles a day." Toasts were made, and so were speeches. Pictures were taken. Reporters scribbled. Waiters served food and drinks to the VIPs while a band played serenades that echoed out across the barren plains. "By mid-morning the following day," writes Brey,

> . . . the train had continued ten miles farther west, where it finally caught up to the construction crews. [Near the present-day freight station of Gannett, on the Union Pacific, 40 miles west of the 100th meridian.] Some hours were spent by the party observing the laying of track, the distribution of material and the general construction process as the tracks grew ever closer to their eventual hook-up with the Western Pacific Railroad. Meanwhile the band played the "Star Spangled Banner," "The Wearing of the Green," "Yankee Doodle," "Rory O'Moore," the "Sprig of Shillalah," etc. Photographic pictures were also taken by the celebrated Viewist, Professor Carbutt of Chicago, of the construction train; and also various groupings of the officers of the road and excursionists.

Then the party headed back east, leaving the workers to their continued labors. For many days thereafter, the newspapers of New York, Boston, Washington, and Chicago were full of accounts of the grand expedition—and how the men of the Union Pacific were confidently taming the continent.

Tunnels, Deserts, and Prairies

As the Union Pacific made swift progress through Nebraska in 1866, the Central Pacific made much slower progress through the rough terrain of the western Sierras. On January 22, 1866, Central Pacific executive Mark Hopkins commented in a letter to Central Pacific president Collis P. Huntington: "It will require all the means and good management that we are master of to build the road over the mountains at the rate we are going." About a month later, in another note, Hopkins described the exorbitantly expensive difficulties of building the road from Dutch Flat in California over the summit and down to the Truckee River, beyond which lay smoother terrain, easier construction, and far more profit per mile on the flat deserts of Nevada. "Snow prevents work about 5–6 months in the year," he wrote, "so we need to get it done this season if possible. . . .

We're pushing hard. For as we see it, it is either a six month job or an eighteen month job to reach a point where the road will earn us a heap and where in construction we can make a pile."

COMPLICATING WEATHER

The winter of 1865–1866 was not kind to the Central Pacific. Precipitation was heavy, and the lower slopes of the Sierras were routinely pelted with torrential rains. The *Sacramento Union* noted that "embankments . . . give way under the soaking rains of this climate, and long delays [in construction] are occasioned." The spongy soil proved impossible with regard to supporting heavy loads. Freight and construction materials simply could not be moved in bulk. At the same time, landslides of saturated earth spread mud, boulders, and the occasional uprooted tree across completed track.

In higher elevations, where the precipitation fell as snow, blizzard-like conditions inhibited the work of blasting and digging out tunnels. A blizzard of five feet fell on New Year's Day, 1866. Spring brought even more snow. Throughout March, sleet and snow came in waves, continuing to the end of May.

As James Strobridge would recall, "The winter made the roads on the clay soils of the foothills nearly impassable for vehicles. The building of the railroad was prosecuted with energy but at a much greater cost than would have been the case in the dry season. . . . All work between Colfax and Dutch Flat was done during this winter in the mud."

All the work was treacherous in this weather, but especially the work of carving and blasting out more than a dozen tunnels, the most perilous of these being the Summit Tunnel located at 7,042 feet above sea level, the highest point reached by the Central Pacific. Engineer Lewis Clement supervised the work at this and most of the other tunnels, where men created the hole using explosive blasts and raw muscle—almost all of it from Chinese workers.

In clearing a path through the Sierra Nevada, the Central Pacific Railroad had to construct more than a dozen tunnels by blasting and boring through the thick rock of this California mountain range. The most perilous of these projects was the 1,659-foot-long Summit Tunnel at Donner Pass, which took more than two years to dig through. Here, laborers remove rocks at the opening of the tunnel.

BRIEF EXPERIMENT WITH NITROGLYCERIN

Chinese workers, by necessity, became experts in the deployment of black powder to blow out holes in mountains. In the process of tunnel making, they frequently used as much as 500 kegs of the powder every day. Because of this high level of demand, the price of the powder rose steadily, starting at around $2.50 per keg and reaching a zenith of $15 per keg by late 1866. This inflation caused Croker, Strobridge, and other supervisors to seek a cheaper alternative, which they soon found in the form of nitroglycerin.

Invented in Italy in 1847 and then refined during the 1860s by Sweden's Alfred Nobel, nitroglycerin packed five times the power of black powder, and was capable of blasts greater than 13 times more earthshaking and earth-moving. However, it was just as dangerous as it was powerful and highly unstable overall. Numerous terrible accidents occurred, with much loss of life, as Chinese workers labored to master the new substance.

Supervisors instructed the workers on how to drill holes 15 inches into the granite walls of the shafts at a slight slant running downhill, pour in the nitro, and then cap the hole with a plug. Once the hole was plugged, the workers triggered the nitro's blast remotely with a percussion cap. But eventually accidents became so numerous—with explosions occurring randomly as the workers gingerly handled the nitro, and also as they banged their picks into accidentally unexploded charges—that the nitro actually began to impede progress of the work rather than advance it. Thus, only at the elevated Summit Tunnel was nitro used for the bulk of the work, and the balance of the tunnels were nearly all blasted out with black powder, regardless of the expense.

EXPLORATION

While the work progressed in the Sierra Nevada in 1866, three bands of surveyors from the Central Pacific poked through various stretches of Nevada, trying to define the optimal route for the railroad to run between the Truckee River's Big Bend (approximately 30 miles from present-day Reno) and the distant Salt Lake Valley, 500 miles to the east. (The most direct route—a straight line—involved traversing a series of mountain ranges. Central Pacific planners were highly desirous of finding an alternative.)

Everywhere, the country seemed inhospitable: a desert littered with the bones of thousands of animals. One surveyor, describing the terrain east of Reno, said that in that area "desolation began to assume its most repulsive form. Miles on miles of black, igneous rock and volcanic detritus. Outcrops

BUILDING THE TUNNELS OF THE SIERRA NEVADA

Writing in *Van Nostrand's Eclectic Engineering Magazine* in 1870, civil engineer John R. Gilliss commented on the tunnels devised and constructed by the men building the Central Pacific through the Sierra Nevada:

During the past summer the track has been completed across this continent, and so much sooner than was thought possible, that the difficulties overcome are apt to be underrated. Some account of a single item in the great work may therefore be interesting.

Between Omaha and Sacramento there are nineteen tunnels. Four of these are on the Union Pacific and fifteen on the Central.

The tunnels of the Central Pacific are nearly all near the summit, where it crosses the western range of the Sierra Nevada. The line here lies on steep hillsides, in some cases being, for long distances, on a face of bare granite, more or less broken by projecting ledges and boulders, but with an average slope often greater than 1 to 1. In such places embankments were almost impracticable; the hills were too steep to catch the slopes, and most of the rock from cuts was thrown far down hill by heavy seam blasts. On these accounts the line, for two miles east of Donner Pass, was thrown further into the hill than on original location, thus adding to the depths of cuttings and increasing the number of tunnels, but saving retaining walls, and where tunnels of lava, interspersed with volcanic grit. . . ." Another potential route, north of the Humboldt River, seemed equally severe and unwelcoming. The river valley route itself, however, seemed to show potential. Surveyor Samuel Bowles, contemplating this thin strip of oasis, insisted that "the Humboldt route would

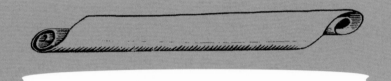

were made, enabling the work to be carried on in winter. Another important object was the saving of snow-covering where tunnels were made, and giving a good foundation for it where they were not. It is within these two miles that seven tunnels are crowded.

Tunnels 1 and 2 are both west of Cisco, a small track 92 miles from Sacramento, and within 13 of the summit. They were both finished in 1866. During the fall of that year the track reached Cisco, and as fast as the gangs of [Chinese workers] were released they were hurried to the summit to be distributed among the tunnels in its vicinity. The year before, some gangs had been sent to summit tunnel No. 6, and commenced the cuts at its extremities; winter set in before the headings were started, and the work had to be abandoned. To avoid a repetition of such delay, the approaches to all the tunnels were covered with men, and worked night and day in three shifts of eight hours each. Thus time was saved, and the tunnel organization started at once. As an illustration of the hurry, I may mention walking two miles over the hills after dark, and staking out the east end of No. 12 by the light of a bonfire; at 9 o'clock the men were at work.

In November and the early part of December there were several snowstorms, just enough to stimulate without delaying the work. The rough rocky sides of Donner Peak soon became smooth, slopes of snow and ice covering the trail that led from tunnel 8 to 9.

be more easily built" than any other route. "It goes through a naturally better country as to wood, water, and fertility of soil. It is generally conceded to be the true natural roadway across the Continent. The emigration has always taken it." With rough deserts and mountains to the north and south, the green corridor of the Humboldt River Valley seemed lush, offering not just water but also excellent grazing and game.

Eventually, the Central Pacific settled on this route. The rail line would run straight due east along the path of the Humboldt until the river rose in northeastern Utah out of the East Humboldt Range, in the so-called Ruby Mountains. From there, the path would go northeast, skirting the desert, and across the Promontory Mountains to an eventual meeting with the Union Pacific. The lines were now drawn.

THE CENTRAL PACIFIC AND THE WINTER OF 1866–1867

As bad as the winter of 1865–1866 had been for the Central Pacific, the winter that followed was even worse. Forty-four individual storms pummeled the workers, many of which involved snowfalls of 10 feet or more. (At Summit Tunnel—where, even today, more snow falls annually than anyplace else in the continental United States—the snow-pack eventually reached 18 feet.) Hundreds of Chinese laborers shoveled snow all day long to keep the mouths of the various tunnels, and the paths to them, open. (Eventually, massive snow tunnels were built leading to the granite tunnels.) Through all this, the option of ceasing operations during the inclement weather was never entertained as a real possibility. With each passing day, Huntington and the other owners of the Central Pacific knew that the Union Pacific was making steady progress through level terrain. The fear of losing all of Nevada and Utah to the Union Pacific inspired Huntington and his cohorts to make their laborers continue to work, even amid the harshest storms.

Accidents and deaths happened with frequency. As J. O. Wilder, a young surveyor, recalled,

> There was one large snowslide at Camp 4, where there were two gangs of Chinese for Tunnels 11 and 12.... The slide took [them] all, and one of the culvert men was not found until the following spring. At our camp the snow was so deep we had to shovel it from the roof and make steps to get to the top. We were snowed in, and our provisions got down to corn meal and tea. Had it lasted one week longer we would have been compelled to eat horse meat, for there were two hundred or more men in my camp.... The cuts were filled by landslides, which had to be removed by gangs of Chinese. A Push Plow loaded with pig-iron to hold it to the rails, with three engines behind, would back up and take a run at the snow and keep going until it got stuck, and then back up and take another run.

Another avalanche near Summit Tunnel killed approximately 20 Chinese workers, whose bodies were not uncovered until spring. According to one contemporary newspaper account, on Christmas Day of 1866, a group of workers were covered by a snow slide, and several died before they could be extracted. Nevertheless, the managers manifested a steely confidence. In the midst of the winter, one of them wrote to Huntington concerning the "terrible storm that has given our RR a severe trial. We do not know the exact extent of the Damage.... Those deep cuts and fills are sliding in and settling." The telegraph line had also collapsed. But "on the whole it has not been as bad as we expected for we had great fears about a good many of the banks and cuts standing a heavy storm. [In fact, the winter may be] the least of our troubles and we no longer fear it. Since the storm I have greater confidence than ever in successfully working our road in the winter."

In the late 1850s, Collis P. Huntington teamed with Mark Hopkins, Leland Stanford, and Charles Crocker to pursue the idea of constructing a rail line to link the eastern and western United States. In 1861, the group formed the Central Pacific Railroad and Huntington served as vice president.

1867

Union Pacific officials upset the leaders of Denver, Colorado, in November 1866, when they made a decision to bypass the city and lay their tracks through the lonesome plains of Wyoming, in the area of Cheyenne, and on to the South Pass through the Rocky Mountains—the path proposed by Jedediah Smith several years before. Union Pacific surveyors did their work in the new terrain throughout the autumn of 1866 and the winter and spring of 1867. Then, in July 1867, land agents associated with the Union Pacific began selling lots adjacent to the projected track route to interested investors. After getting off to a dismal start laying just 40 miles of track in 1865, the Union Pacific had a much better year in 1866, putting down some 260 miles of rail all told. The year 1867, however, saw the mileage drop down to 240.

As usual, surveyors were in the forefront of the activity. Union Pacific surveyor Thomas Hubbard, busy drawing a line across Wyoming during early August 1867, wrote revealing notes in his journal. On August 5, he wrote, "The country over which we passed was a barren desert of alkali composition. There was not a spear of grass or a drop of water in the whole distance." On August 6, he entered, "Run about ten times and quit work at six P.M. The country through which we run was if possible more barren than yesterday. There is no water with in ten miles of our line. We have to haul our water in barrels. The team started tonight to get a fresh supply. The weather is suffocatingly hot." And on August 7, Hubbard added, "The team returned with casks filled with water. But it was so full of all kinds of poison that we could not use it. It was as red as blood and filled with all kinds of vermin. The horses and mules as dry as they are would not drink it. We were compelled to return twenty miles to our old camp to get water."

When, that summer, Union Pacific surveyors extended their reach into Weber Canyon, near Salt Lake City, they bumped into Central Pacific surveyors approaching the same landscape from the opposite direction. Both railroads had designs on the potentially lucrative Mormon business in Utah, and both were planning their route. Time would tell as to which railroad would eventually come to dominate the

Utah Territory, but both had ambitions and both had designs. The Union Pacific had the edge, because all that lay between Laramie, Wyoming, and Utah was relatively flat open space: the Great Basin. "The work of building the road there was

A VIEW OF THE CENTRAL PACIFIC "END OF TRACK"

In August 1868, a *San Francisco Times* reporter wrote the following words on the state of travel and construction of the Central Pacific at the end of track, some 250 miles east of Sacramento. The article was reprinted by the editor of the *Carson Daily Appeal*, Henry R. Mighels, on August 27, 1868:

As we approached our destination we passed several white tents. . . . Further on was a camp of [Chinese workers], who were at this time employed in cooking their mid-day meal. All along the road were scattered heaps of ties, fish plates, spikes and other material. Still more white tents, and then numbers of heavy wagons, prairie schooners in fact, which are employed in hauling the ties, and then a strange looking affair which resembles a good-sized street upon wheels. This is the Boarding Train. It consists of some six or eight huge cars, or rather houses built upon car trucks. Four of these are dormitories for the white laborers; others are used as eating houses; others again as kitchens; one is appropriated to the family of Mr. Strowbridge [sic], the engineer in charge of construction, and another is occupied by Mr. Menkier, the General Superintendent, Mr. Vandenburg, the Telegraph Superintendent, and some of the overseers and other officers in charge of the works. In this train they live, eat, and sleep, and it is moved forward day by day as the road advances. The Chinese laborers, who have Superintendents of their own, of course under the general supervision of the white officers, reside in camps by themselves, and

unexpectedly light," Grenville Dodge would write many years later, "and it almost seems that nature made this great opening in the Rocky Mountains expressly for the passage of a transcontinental railway."

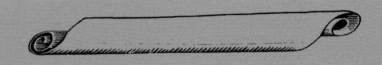

being divided into two shifts, or gangs, are moved alternately every other day. The scene at the front is almost as exciting as a battle. Trains are continually arriving, loaded with wooden ties and iron rails, and being unloaded with marvelous rapidity, are sent back to Wadsworth for fresh supplies. Heretofore the difficulties in the way of transportation have been so great that it has been impossible to supply the tracklayers with sufficient material, and their powers of work have really never been fairly tested, until last week, when they laid six miles and eight hundred feet in one day.

The first thing that strikes the visitor on arriving at the front is the amazing energy and activity displayed by every one connected with the road. It is not only in the superintendents and engineers that this feature is noticeable. It pervades the whole army of workmen, from the wiry foreman, whose intelligent features have been tanned nearly black by the burning sun, to the swarthy [Chinese worker], who speaks no word of the language of his employers. There is no such thing as shirking or grumbling known among these men. . . . Of the white laborers we may say that we never saw a finer body of their class. They are all picked men—hale, strong and sober. There are now about four thousand men employed in grading the road, and this party is more than fifty miles ahead of the tracklayers. They have smooth and easy ground to work upon at present, and being subjected to no delays from the lack of material, are enabled to push forward at a rate of from three to five miles a day.

As for the progress of the Central Pacific, Strobridge and his crew continued work on the Summit Tunnel and other tunnels through the spring and summer of 1867, finally breaking through in August. The tunnel was 1,659 feet in length, and at its deepest point, reached 124 feet down into the granite of the Sierra Nevada. By November 30, the grading was done through the tunnel, and the track laid, the final spikes put in place. Also on that day, the first scheduled train from Sacramento showed up. "Yesterday," Mark Hopkins wrote Huntington on the thirty-first, "we all went up to see the first locomotive pass the summit of the Sierra. It was a pleasant sight to reach such a point where a train would gravitate towards the East. For these years past gravitation has been so continually against us that at times it seemed to me that it would have been well if we had practiced a while on smaller and shorter hills before attacking so huge a mountain. . . . [Now] we are on the down grade & we rejoice. The operators and laborers all rejoice. All work freer and with more spirit."

The Great Race

The race between the Central Pacific and the Union Pacific began in earnest after the Central Pacific left the Sierra Nevada, into Nevada, and after the Union Pacific emerged out of Nebraska, into Wyoming. By then, officials of both rail lines realized they were most likely destined to meet somewhere in the Mormon territory of Utah: But the question was where—how far to the east and how far to the west—and which company would, in the end, lay claim to the most real estate and miles of track.

Writing in the summer of 1868, a Nevada reporter observing the construction of the Central Pacific commented: "The gap in the great span or iron that shall wed the two oceans is decreasing day by day.... No longer is the long and drowsy journey by the way of Panama deemed safe or expeditious by the busy man whose time is as coin to him.... The long and tedious stage ride grows less each day.... The overland route is preferable even in winter for all practical purposes of travel. Every day sees a huge train of sixty cars laden with timber, ties and railway iron pass Reno on its way to 'the front.'" Writing that same summer, a reporter for the *Chicago Leader* noted: "Old men, who predicted that the road would be built, but 'not in our time,' may have an opportunity of bathing in the Atlantic one week and in the Pacific the next—or sleigh-riding in New York on Christmas, and pulling ripe oranges in Los Angeles on New Years."

As the Nevada reporter observed, travelers were already making use of the Transcontinental Railroad, even though it was not yet finished. Riders going west to east or east to west took either the Union Pacific or the Central Pacific to the ends of the lines, and then used a stagecoach to navigate the constantly shrinking distance that lay between the two spits of rail.

PARALLEL ROADS

A clause of the later version of the Pacific Railway Act allowed both the Union Pacific and the Central Pacific to grade 300 miles in advance of the track already laid and to collect part of the government bonds allocated for the mileage. Thus, Grenville Dodge and Thomas Durant entered 1868 hoping to lay their track within 100 miles of Ogden, Utah, before the end of the year, a strategic position that would allow them to send their grading crews all the way to Humboldt Wells, Nevada. Huntington and the other executives of the Central Pacific, on the other hand, hoped also to get to Ogden in the same time frame: a strategic position that would allow them to push their grades all the way into Wyoming.

Again, Dodge and Durant had the edge here. The first 150 miles after Cheyenne offered relatively easy countryside as opposed to what the Central Pacific faced, yet the government promised to deliver the Union Pacific $48,000 in bonds for each mile of track. (From Omaha to Cheyenne, the Union Pacific had received just $16,000 in bonds per mile. Upon reaching the Great Basin in Utah, the firm would garner $32,000 in bonds per mile.) The Central Pacific was looking at similar bond economics, but a dramatically different landscape. That spring found the Central Pacific's track ending at Donner Lake in California, several hundred miles short of Humboldt Wells.

The Central Pacific's leaders were, however, undaunted. During the spring of 1868, Collis P. Huntington made an audacious bid. He sent a fictitious report to Secretary of the Interior Orville Hickman Browning that said the Central Pacific track was approaching Humboldt Wells, and asked permission to begin grading to the north of Salt Lake, across the Promontory Mountains to Ogden, and north and east of the Wasatch Range. In the end, on May 15, the secretary—based on Huntington's assertions—approved Huntington's proceeding as far as Monument Point, Utah. Huntington was unapologetic in explaining the deceit to his colleagues, for he believed that absolutely everything in the way of success was contingent upon proceeding with the grading. "It is a very important matter," Huntington wrote Leland Stanford. "We should be bold and take and hold possession of the line [as far as we can]."

Meanwhile, the Union Pacific proceeded to survey as far ahead as it possibly could and to grade accordingly. In due course, the railroads were making parallel grades just a few miles apart from each other, work that was entirely redundant.

SHERMAN SUMMIT

One of the Union Pacific's first major projects in the spring of 1868 was the bridging of Sherman Summit, above Dale Creek in Wyoming. When preparations for building the bridge were in full swing that spring, a reporter for the *Cheyenne Daily Leader* said that "a vast and varied amount of freight and passengers went to the end of track today. There were five car loads of iron and spikes, twenty-five dirt scrapers, twenty quarters

One of the Union Pacific's first major construction projects was bridging Sherman Summit, which is located between Cheyenne and Laramie in Wyoming. The 650-foot-long trestle rises 150 feet above Dale Creek and was completed in April 1868.

of fresh beef, patent plows, men's boots, gunnies of ham, cases of pepper-sauce, sacks of grain, bales of clothing, and working men with Winchester rifles, carpet bags, blankets and every other conceivable article of tools, food, and wearing apparel."

Wood for the bridge was cut in Michigan and then taken to a Chicago workshop, where artisans fashioned it into double-framed trestles with massive bents 40 feet apart. Once ready, it came by rail to the end of track at the brink of Dale Creek. The bridge was half-finished when, on April 14, a mighty storm descended. "Wind blowing a gale," wrote Union Pacific engineer Samuel Reed, "no work being done on bridge. Do not ship the truss bridges until further orders." Another engineer, Hezekiah Bissell, commented further, describing the brutal winds that threatened the fledgling structure: "The bridge men were scared out of their wits and doing nothing to save the thing." Bissell took charge, telling them "to bring every rope and chain they could get hold of to the bridge as soon as possible. When the ropes first came, no one dared to go and put them on to guy [steady] the bridge. I finally induced two or three to go, and soon there were plenty of others. I probably saved the bridge."

Two days later, the bridge stood complete over Sherman Summit. Top Union Pacific executives—including Durant and Dodge—came to watch the first train go across. Durant himself personally drove the final spike on the last rail of the summit. And Dodge himself telegraphed the eastern newspapers: "The Union Pacific Rail Road crossed the Summit of the mountains this day, the highest elevation reached by any railroad in the world."

THE WILD AND AWFUL HORRORS OF THE WEST

After Sherman Summit, Union Pacific managers set their sites on making a minimum of three miles per day in laid track, with graders 300 miles out making the same progress. "I have never been hurried up more in my life," John Casement wrote his wife. "Have crossed the high Bridge [Sherman Summit] today and want to commence laying three miles a day at once." The path was downhill, down the western slope of the Black Hills, and in only a few days they made it to Laramie and had grade

(continues on page 88)

STANFORD, HUNTINGTON, HOPKINS, AND CROCKER

Leaders of the Central Pacific Railroad

In his "Story of the Central Pacific," published in the January and February 1908 issues of *The Pacific Monthly*, W. F. Bailey described the gentlemen who formed the nucleus of the Central Pacific Railroad at the time of its founding in 1861:

> Mr. Huntington was a Connecticut Yankee, quick-sighted, cool and with few equals as a business man in Sacramento, where his opinions carried great weight. He despised nothing that had a dollar's profit in it for him. In the conduct of the future affairs of the road to him fell naturally the financial end of their deals—the negotiation of loans, floating of securities, purchase of materials and supplies and their dispatch from the East, establishing his office in New York City in 1864 the better to accomplish this. If there was a dominant influence in their organization it was exercised by him.
>
> Through Huntington five other Sacramentans were induced to join the syndicate. These were Leland Stanford, then Governor of California and a leader of the Republican party just coming into power. A lawyer, diplomatic and popular, he had had some little experience and practical knowledge in construction work, having served with his father, who had been a railroad and canal contractor in the East. His was the part of diplomacy.
>
> Another was Charles Crocker, a self-made man, remarkable for his energy, of strong physique and will power, fearless and earnest, one of the leading merchants of Sacramento, with several branch stores in the interior. He had had considerable

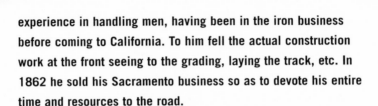

experience in handling men, having been in the iron business before coming to California. To him fell the actual construction work at the front seeing to the grading, laying the track, etc. In 1862 he sold his Sacramento business so as to devote his entire time and resources to the road.

Mark Hopkins, the fourth member of this remarkably strong organization, was also a merchant, in Sacramento, the next-door neighbor and warm personal friend of Huntington, known to his friends as "Uncle Mark" and described by one of them as "the truest and best man that ever lived." His inclinations and abilities ran in the direction of inside or office work; methodical, accurate and painstaking, the natural man to handle the company's finances.

These constituted the syndicate that raised the $35,000 necessary to carry on the work which was pushed ahead under [Theodore] Judah's supervision during the summer of 1861.

On June 28 of that year these, together with D. W. Strong, of Dutch Flat, and Charles Marsh, of Nevada City, California, organized the Central Pacific Railroad Company of California, with a capital stock of $8,500,000—85,000 shares of a par value of $100 each. The original subscriptions were $150 each, by Stanford, Huntington, Hopkins, Judah, and Crocker, and 730 shares by all others, in all 1,480 shares, par value $148,000, thus just bringing them within the limits as set by the laws of California, which required that $1,000 worth of stock be subscribed for each mile of road contemplated.

---

* Full text of the article is available online at
   http://www.cprr.org/Museum/Bailey_CPRR_1908.html

After Union Pacific workers reached Laramie, Wyoming, in June 1868, they then turned due north to Rock Creek, where the line again headed west toward Utah. Pictured here is the Laramie Hotel in 1869, shortly after the Union Pacific tracks were constructed.

(continued from page 85)
work done through more than half the distance of Wyoming, culminating at Green River.

As Stephen Ambrose writes, "The grade went nearly straight north out of Laramie. Then, just past Rock Creek it turned straight west across the Medicine Bow River, up to and across the North Platte River. Fort Steele was on the western side of the North Platte River, then, a bit farther west, a town founded by the Union Pacific and called Benton, then Rawlins Springs [today called Rawlins]. The most important work, after the

Dale Creek Bridge was operating, was to get the bridge up and the tracks . . . ready for trains at the crossing of the North Platte River."

This was accomplished through late May, June, and into early July—all under harassment from Indian parties. In addition to harassing the construction crews, the Indians were also intent on stealing the cattle that traveled with the crews as a food source. Entries from the bridge construction foreman's diary tell the tale. On May 24, he wrote, "The Indians made a dash on some pilgrims who camped on the opposite side of the river and succeeded in capturing 19 head of stock." On June 4, he entered, "At about sunrise, were attacked by Indians and succeeded in shooting one." June 21 had this entry: "Indians killed two men. Both had been horribly mutilated about the face by cuts made by a knife or a tomahawk. They captured one hundred head of stock."

In the end, the men of the Union Pacific wound up despising the Native Americans. "I have no sympathy for the red devils," wrote one construction engineer, "notwithstanding the halo of romance by which they are surrounded by the people of the East, who, secure in their happy and peaceful homes, know naught the wild and awful horrors of the West. . . . Let the savage strength of the demonic Indian be broken. May their dwelling places and habitations be destroyed. May the greedy crow hover over their silent corpses. May the coyote feast upon their stiff and festering carcasses, and the sooner the better."

Despite these depredations visited on the railroad workers by the Indians, the bridge over the North Platte River was finished by July 15. The first three trains to cross over were all construction trains, carrying freight cars packed with rails, ties, and other necessary items. The first passenger train came through on the twenty-first. And the work continued in earnest. By early November, the end of track could be pinpointed on the map 890 miles west of Omaha, and John Casement reported to his bosses that he was "straining every nerve to get into Salt Lake Valley before the heavy snows fall. Thirty more days of good weather will let us do it." Meanwhile, back in Omaha, another crew worked to build an enormous railroad bridge across the Missouri, connecting Council Bluffs and Omaha: in other words, connecting New York and Boston with Omaha.

RACING TO OGDEN

What drove the Casements, Durant, Dodge, and all the other leaders of the Union Pacific was an intense desire not only to get to Ogden, Utah, before the Central Pacific, but also—if possible—to push well beyond Ogden to Humboldt Wells or even farther west. This ambitious plan absolutely required that the Union Pacific lay track through Echo Canyon, Utah, and down to Ogden itself before the winter of 1868–1869 set in. "How fast are you sending men to head of Echo?" Durant demanded to know of John Casement on December 18. "We want 2,000 as soon as can be had."

Meanwhile, the *Salt Lake Daily Reporter* carried an item in its pages indicating that "the Union Pacific has four locating parties, and two construction parties of engineers [in the area between the north end of the Salt Lake and Humboldt Wells], while the Central Pacific Company also has six parties of engineers between the same points. We understand that the lines of the two companies are being run nearly parallel, and everything now seems to indicate that there will be two grades if not two roads, between the Lake and the Wells."

Helping the Union Pacific make this progress were hundreds of Mormon workers. The Union Pacific—through negotiations with Mormon leader Brigham Young—arranged for Mormons to do much of the grading between the head of Echo Canyon and Salt Lake. The Union Pacific provided the tools, resources, surveyors, and supervision, while the Mormons provided the able-bodied young men. In exchange for the Mormons' assistance, the Union Pacific paid 30¢ per cubit yard for excavations where earth needed to be hauled less than 200 feet, and 50¢ for hauls beyond 200 feet. The Mormons also did tunneling at $15 a yard. On top of this, the Union Pacific paid Young and the Mormon Church—not the workers—$2 and up a day per worker, depending on skill. In the midst of a grasshopper blight that was killing much of the wheat crop in Utah, most Mormon young men were happy to get the work.

Shortly after engaging with the Union Pacific, Brigham Young—a sharp businessman—engaged as well with the Central Pacific. In November 1868, Young contracted with the Central Pacific to build grade from Ogden (a bit north of Salt Lake City) west to Monument Point. When the Mormons employed by the Central Pacific set to work, they found themselves grading within shouting range of workers for the Union Pacific, both crews navigating the long line between Weber Canyon and Humboldt Wells.

Collis P. Huntington prayed for early snow and for the Union Pacific crew following the graders with track to get bogged down in Weber Canyon for the duration of the winter. "One good storm," he wrote Mark Hopkins on December 10, "would settle the question of their coming through the Weber Canyon this winter." In the end, however, freezing conditions came before snow. Before the end of the year, a writer for the *Salt Lake Daily Reporter* noted: "Notwithstanding the Herculean efforts made by both companies, work may have to be suspended on a large portion yet to be done. The elements are obstacles which even railroad enterprise and energy sometimes cannot overcome."

Once again, the competing crews laid down their tools and began several frustrating months of waiting out the winter, contemplating spring, and anticipating the recommencement of the great race. "Next season," Huntington wrote a colleague, "will decide much, and perhaps *all*. Next season we shall see just where our bread is or isn't buttered. Count on it."

Finale

Through early 1869, both companies faced numerous hurdles—geographical and financial—as they sprinted toward completion of the Transcontinental Railroad.

FINANCIAL AND SUPPLY ISSUES

The Union Pacific spent the bulk of its available funds pushing quickly through Nebraska and Wyoming in 1868. As 1869 loomed and work progressed in Utah, the firm found itself stretched for cash to pay the Mormons and other laborers on whose goodwill the rapid continuation of the line depended. In fact, the firm found itself $10 million in debt. How could this be? Because the Crédit Mobilier stood in the middle between the government bonds and the real work of developing the railroad, flagrantly siphoning off funds.

Soon, Brigham Young himself had to start writing collection letters to the Union Pacific's Durant, in an attempt to collect $750,000 in back wages for the Mormon workers. "To say the least," Young wrote Durant, this is "strange treatment of my account after the exertions made to put the grading through for the Company. It is not for myself that I urge, but for the thousands who have done the work." Few disinterested observers had any illusions about the corruption in the upper management of the Union Pacific, a firm that paid nearly 300 percent in dividends in one year to wealthy investors, but could not—or would not—pay honest wages owed to employees.

The Central Pacific had similar cash-flow problems and similar graft issues, with contracts moving through Huntington, Hopkins, and Crocker's Contract and Finance Company before flowing down to subcontractors. But they also had supply issues. "We have in Ca. 183 miles iron and only 89 miles spikes," Crocker telegraphed Huntington near the end of January 1869, "and 81 miles iron and 75 miles spikes to arrive in sixty days. It is very unsafe to half-spike the track at this season of the year." Such problems of getting enough raw material in hand, and then getting it promptly to the end of track, were to dog the Central Pacific for the balance of the project. The Union Pacific, on the other hand, had relatively clear lines of supply distribution—if only they could pay their workers.

SAVAGE WEATHER

Weather once again conspired against the project in the first months of 1869, as both firms continued to build throughout the winter and to do so in haste. As Stephen Ambrose described,

> At Humboldt Wells, Nevada, and to the east into Utah, where Strobridge's graders were at work, temperatures went to eighteen degrees below zero in mid-January and stayed that low

for a week. By the end of the cold spell, the soil was frozen solid to a depth of nearly two feet. The graders could not use their picks or shovels. Instead, they blew up the frozen ground with black powder. The explosion split the earth into big pieces. And these pieces were then assembled into make-shift grades which Crocker derided as being nothing more than "chunks of ice." In the spring, according to Crocker, "this all melted and down went the track. It was almost impossible to get a train over it without getting off the track."

Storms also harassed the workers of the Union Pacific. An early January snowstorm in Wyoming covered the entire track already laid and the entire grade awaiting track. A freight train headed for Echo, Utah, worked 14 hours through the drifts in order to cover just 40 miles of territory. On the heels of the snow came blistering cold, with temperatures descending to 20 degrees below zero. Like their counterparts with the Central Pacific, the Union Pacific graders resorted to blasting the frozen ground—with equally dismal results to follow in the spring. Then in February came what one Salt Lake City newspaper called "the most terrific storm for years." More than 90 miles of Union Pacific track between Rawlins and Laramie, Wyoming, had to be shut down for three weeks. Eastbound passengers—more than 200 of them—found themselves marooned in Rawlins, and 600 westbound passengers spent unhappy weeks in Laramie. (The eastbound passengers were mostly headed from California to Washington, D.C., for the inauguration of the newly elected president, Ulysses S. Grant. In the end, they missed the party.)

Working in frigid temperatures and in haste, construction crews on both railroads did second- and third-rate work. The future economist Henry George—at the time a reporter for the *Sacramento Union*—rode over some of the winter track laid by the Central Pacific men the following April and commented

Although several thousand supporters attended President Ulysses S. Grant's inauguration on March 4, 1869, many who were traveling from California to Washington, D.C., missed the celebration. In February of that year, a massive snowstorm hit Wyoming and 200 eastbound Union Pacific passengers were stranded in the town of Rawlins for three weeks.

that it seemed to have been "thrown together in the biggest kind of hurry."

Accidents—the result of shabby work compounded by the severe winter weather—seemed inevitable. A Central Pacific construction train became uncoupled as it was going down the long grade out of the mountains into Reno. Although the front half of the train got well ahead, the uncoupled back half eventually gained enough momentum to slam into the first, crushing two brakemen. On the Union Pacific's side, an engine straining to plow through the dense drifting snow of a February storm had its boiler explode, killing an engineer, fireman, and conductor, along with a brakeman who was crushed when a car overturned as a result of the explosion.

THE APRIL COMPROMISE

February 16 found the Central Pacific 20 miles east of Humboldt Wells, Nevada, and the Union Pacific 20 miles east of Ogden, Utah. Thirteen days later, the Central Pacific had laid down another 20 miles. Although they were almost into Utah, they were still 144 miles from Promontory Summit, the approximated meeting point with the Union Pacific. On the other hand, the Union Pacific was—by the end of February—just 66 miles from Promontory, having laid track to Devil's Gate Bridge on the Weber River, six miles from the mouth of Weber Canyon.

Meanwhile, grading, fill, and bridge work had already begun in the area of Promontory. The summit itself presented significant logistical hurdles for both companies. While the summit basin offered hospitable and easy landscape, getting up to the summit basin from both east and west was a challenge. The Union Pacific faced large, projecting limestone abutments that needed to be done away with and deep ravines requiring either bridges or filling. The Central Pacific faced equally problematic issues. One fill that the Central Pacific worked on in the vicinity of Promontory demanded no less than 10,000 yards of earth— and 500 workers along with 250 teams of horses, laboring for a full three months.

"The race," Grenville Dodge wrote a friend on March 23, "is getting exciting and interesting." It was interesting in Utah, and interesting in Washington, D.C., where legislators had taken notice of parallel work being done by the competing railroads and began to agitate for a cutting off of funds until the final meeting of the stalemated railroads was assured.

With this possibility ahead of them, Dodge and Huntington sat down together on April 9, when they formally agreed that the roads would meet at Promontory, northwest of Ogden, with the Central Pacific building to Promontory and then purchasing the Union Pacific's track as far as Ogden. That same evening, the Congress of the United States made it official and thus put an end to the "race" between the Union Pacific and the Central Pacific. The joint resolution of Congress said, in part, "The common terminus of the Union Pacific and the Central Pacific railroads shall be at or near Ogden, and the Union Pacific Railroad Company shall build, and the Central Pacific Railroad Company shall pay for and own, the railroad from the terminus aforesaid to Promontory Summit, at which the rails shall meet and connect and form one continuous line." Putting Congress's words into action, on April 10, the Union Pacific's workers stopped grading west of Promontory, and on April 15, the Central Pacific's workers stopped grading east of Promontory.

FINAL PUSH

Nevertheless, a certain element of rivalry continued between the two companies. This was felt especially among the men of the Union Pacific who—in their work building between Ogden and Promontory—suddenly felt relegated to mere contractors for the Central Pacific. Every grade they made, every rail they laid, and every spike they drove would soon be handed over to the Central Pacific, and this impacted morale. Up to this point, Union Pacific workers had rather glumly kept working when pay was late—as it frequently was. But Dodge guessed this would not continue to be the case, given the new set of circumstances. "Men will work no longer without pay," he wrote Oliver Ames, "and stoppage now is fatal to us." John Casement also wrote to headquarters to say that merchants and suppliers from Omaha to Ogden were "loaded with UPRR paper [debt] and if the company don't send some money here soon they will bust up the whole country." Shortly, Ames fielded yet another urgent telegram from Utah: "We must have five hundred thousand to pay contractors men immediately or road cannot run."

On April 28, the Central Pacific set a record by grading and laying 10 miles and 56 feet of track in one day—the effort being made to facilitate a bet between Durant and Crocker. Crocker's $10,000 said the Central Pacific could rise to the occasion and lay down at least 10 miles in a day. Durant's $10,000 said they could not. On the twenty-eighth, the Central Pacific crews worked with several Union Pacific observers on hand. Tellingly, even though the Central Pacific men accomplished the task, Durant never paid Crocker the $10,000.

Concurrent with this, according to the *Alta California* newspaper's correspondent at Promontory, "the Union Pacific road creeps on but slowly; they had to build a tremendous trestle-work, over 400 feet long and 85 feet high. But their rock cutting is the most formidable work, and it seems a pity that such a big job should be necessary." Standing atop Promontory, the reporter could see the broad reach of construction across the landscape, the Union Pacific crews to the east and the Central Pacific crews to the west. "Along the line of the road may be seen the white [tent] camps of the Chinese laborers, and from every one of them squads of these people are advancing." Finally, on April 30, the Central Pacific crews reached the end of what they had to build. "The last blow has been struck on the Central Pacific Railroad," wrote the *Alta California* correspondent, "and the last tie and rail were placed in position today. We are now waiting for the Union Pacific to finish their rock-cutting."

As the two lines came nearer and nearer to one another, the number of men required in the building steadily diminished. As of May 3, both the Union Pacific and the Central Pacific embarked upon massive layoffs. The *Alta California* reporter noted the teams of workers "melting away" and said, "the white camps which dotted every brown hillside and every shady glen . . . are being broken up and abandoned. The Central Pacific force is nearly all gone already, and that of the Union is going fast. Ninety of the latter left for the East this

On May 10, 1869, the Union Pacific and Central Pacific railroads met at Promontory Summit, Utah, thus linking the eastern railroad network with California. This wood engraving, which appeared in the June 5, 1869, issue of *Harper's Weekly*, depicts the engineers of the two lines shaking hands at the point where the two trains came together.

morning, and a hundred more go tomorrow, and the rest will soon follow."

AFTERWARDS

Following the Golden Spike celebration that occurred at Promontory Summit on May 10, 1869, the few remaining workers disbanded. The bulk of the Irish laborers headed east, and the bulk of the Chinese workers headed west to the California coast. Soon enough, the crucial role of the Chinese would be forgotten.

During 1882, Congress enacted the Chinese Exclusion Act, banning Chinese immigration to the United States for 10 years. The law would be extended twice: in 1892 and in 1904.

GEORGE PULLMAN
(1831–1897)

Traveling the Transcontinental Railroad

One of the first passengers to travel the length of the finished Transcontinental Railroad from Omaha to Sacramento was George Pullman, who did so to advertise the luxuries of his Pullman Palace Car, a railroad sleeping car. As part of his publicity blitz, Pullman wrote a detailed account of his journey, which was published in the *New York Times* on June 28, 1869:

We reached Green River (846 miles west of Omaha) at noon of Tuesday, and from this point on, the country begins to be a little less absolutely abandoned to the Fiend [Pullman's phrase for Native Americans]. We are now past the rocky ridge, which forms the divide of the continent, and henceforth all the running waters go to seek the Pacific Ocean. Green River is itself grateful to the eye, and has here and there picturesque banks and touches of verdure that seem of ravishing beauty.

Later in the afternoon you pass a wonderfully striking and picturesque succession of architectural hills or buttes, where nature seems to have sought to exhaust herself in all manner of fantastic forms of castles, cathedrals and pyramids, crumbling and majestic, fashioned, perhaps, by the Titans in some sportive mood. From this [point] on the mountains grow bolder and more precipitous, and fold in closer and closer around you, till finally they break into wondrous canyons, narrow and rugged. The first of these is Echo Canyon

It is recorded that in 1880, the Union Pacific and Central Pacific combined carried an average of $50 million in freight annually. In addition, the Union Pacific served as the first

(993 miles from Omaha) and, farther on, Weber Canyon (1,008 miles from Omaha). It was 10 o'clock Tuesday night before we reached Echo, so we had little opportunity to see these striking objects. Yet if the vision was obscured, the darkness served to intensify their weird and wild grandeur. . . . We awoke early Wednesday morning to find ourselves at Promontory, the western terminus of the Union Pacific Railroad, the eastern commencement of the Central Pacific. We had made the long stretch of 1,084 miles in a little over sixty hours.

As we have passed over the whole of the Union Pacific Railroad, this might be the proper place to enter into some reflections on the character of the road, as a road. . . . For near a thousand miles it is as good as could possibly be desired. The last hundred or hundred and fifty miles we passed over when we were asleep; but when we compared notes in the morning, we could not discover that this part of the track had been rough enough to disturb in the least our slumbers. I suppose, however, I have from the officers of the road a pretty accurate conception of the character of this part of the Union Pacific. The track was laid before the frost was out of the ground, and when the thaw came it was left in a bad condition of ballast.

From Promontory westward there is a long stretch of several hundred miles which is one dreary monotone of sage-brush and desolation. . . . The railroad follows the Humboldt Valley for 250 miles—a valley walled in to the north by high volcanic table-lands, and presenting but little of interest in all its wide stretch.

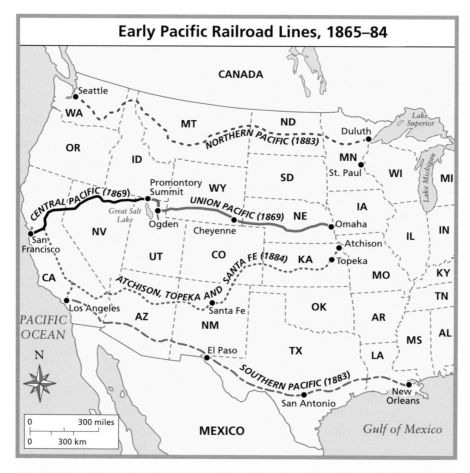

Early Pacific Railroad Lines, 1865–84

By the end of the nineteenth century, much of the West was accessible via rail line. This map shows the primary railroads of the West, with the Union Pacific and Central Pacific lines in bold.

choice in transport for migrants intent on settling the lands west of the Missouri River. As a consequence of that settlement, by the mid-1880s, virtually all the Plains Indians of the West found themselves in a state of surrender, consigned to reservations. The buffalo they had once hunted, and which once populated the West by the millions, had by that time been overhunted to such an extent by the white settlers that a mere 1,000 roamed the plains.

During 1872 and 1873, the emerging scandal of the Crédit Mobilier eventually brought shame to many of the politicians associated with the Union Pacific and revealed the fraud that had been rampant throughout the construction of the railroad. Twenty years later, in 1892, Union Pacific executive Sidney Dillon recalled that at the completion of the Transcontinental Railroad, he and other leaders of both the Union Pacific and the Central Pacific "were strongly impressed with the conviction that the event was of historic importance; but, as I remember it now, we connected it rather with the notion of transcontinental communication and trade with China and Japan than with internal development, or what railroad men call local traffic." Dillon went on to say that while not one of his colleagues was disappointed "in the tremendous results attained" by the Transcontinental Railroad, "they are different from those we looked for, and of vastly greater consequence for the country." Indeed, Asian trade produced only 5 percent of the railroad's business in 1891 versus the 95 percent that was homegrown—statistics that make clear just how vital a tool for growth the railroad became.

CHRONOLOGY

1861   **June** Collis P. Huntington, Charles Crocker, Leland Stanford, and Mark Hopkins incorporate the Central Pacific Railroad in California.

1862   **July** President Abraham Lincoln signs into law the "Act to Aid in the Construction of a Railroad and Telegraph Line from the Missouri River to the Pacific Ocean"—also known as the Pacific Railway Act of 1862—establishing the Union Pacific

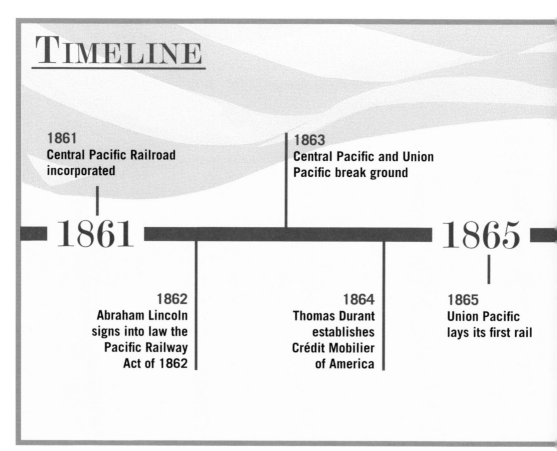

TIMELINE

1861
Central Pacific Railroad incorporated

1863
Central Pacific and Union Pacific break ground

1861

1865

1862
Abraham Lincoln signs into law the Pacific Railway Act of 1862

1864
Thomas Durant establishes Crédit Mobilier of America

1865
Union Pacific lays its first rail

Railroad and authorizing this entity to partner with the Central Pacific in completing a transcontinental railroad, and providing financing for the same.

1863   **January** The Central Pacific breaks ground in Sacramento, California.

1863   **December** The Union Pacific breaks ground near Council Bluffs, Iowa, and Omaha, Nebraska, on either side of the Missouri River.

1864   The Union Pacific's Thomas Durant establishes the Crédit Mobilier of America and, with the Central Pacific's Collis Huntington, helps get the Pacific

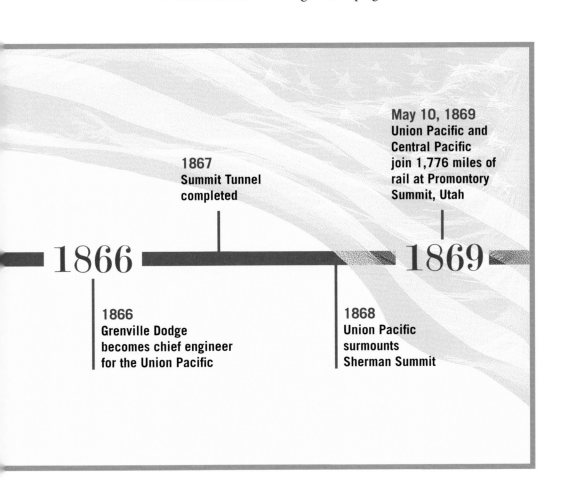

1867
Summit Tunnel
completed

May 10, 1869
Union Pacific and
Central Pacific
join 1,776 miles of
rail at Promontory
Summit, Utah

1866   1869

1866
Grenville Dodge
becomes chief engineer
for the Union Pacific

1868
Union Pacific
surmounts
Sherman Summit

Railway Act of 1864 through Congress, providing both railroads with more generous federal subsidies than the 1862 act.

Early 1865 Labor shortages in California force Central Pacific general superintendent Charles Crocker and Construction Superintendent James H. Strobridge to employ Chinese laborers.

1865 **July** The Union Pacific lays its first rail at Omaha, and the Central Pacific reaches a point 50 miles east of Sacramento.

1866 **April** Brothers John and Dan Casement are hired to oversee Union Pacific construction teams.

1866 **May** Grenville Dodge signs on as chief engineer for the Union Pacific.

1866 **August** Union Pacific track reaches 150 miles west of Omaha.

1866 **October** Union Pacific track reaches the 100th meridian, nearly 250 miles west of Omaha.

1866 **November** Central Pacific track reaches Cisco, 92 miles east of Sacramento, and the Union Pacific track reaches North Platte, 290 miles west of Omaha.

1867 **November** The Central Pacific finishes Summit Tunnel, an incredible feat of engineering, more than 7,000 feet above sea level.

1867 **December 13** The Central Pacific lays its first track in Nevada; the first rails are laid eastward across the Nevada line, having bypassed a 17-mile stretch of track in the Donner Lake area.

Early 1868   Mormon leader Brigham Young contracts with both the Union Pacific and Central Pacific to build grade in Utah; the Central Pacific track reaches Reno, Nevada, and the Union Pacific starts construction west of Cheyenne, Wyoming.

1868   **April 16** The Union Pacific surmounts Sherman Summit, more than 8,000 feet above sea level.

1868   **May** Union Pacific extends its track as far as Laramie, Wyoming.

1868   **July** Central Pacific track extends to Wadsworth, Nevada.

1868   **September** Central Pacific track reaches to Mill City, Nevada.

1868   **November** Union Pacific track reaches to Bear River in Utah.

1869   **March** Union Pacific workers drive the last spike extending the railroad to Ogden, Utah.

1869   **April** Grenville Dodge of the Union Pacific and Collis P. Huntington of the Central Pacific formally agree to join their tracks in the vicinity of Promontory, Utah.

1869   **April 30** The Central Pacific track reaches Promontory.

1869   **May 7** The Union Pacific track reaches Promontory.

1869   **May 10** Golden Spike Ceremony marks the completion of the Transcontinental Railroad at Promontory Summit in Utah.

1957   **April 2** Golden Spike National Historic Site opens.

1965   **July 30** Golden Spike becomes part of National Park Service.

BIBLIOGRAPHY

Ahearn, Robert G. *Union Pacific Country*. Lincoln: University of Nebraska Press, 1971.

Ambrose, Stephen. *Nothing Like It in the World: The Men Who Built the Transcontinental Railroad 1863–1869*. New York: Simon & Schuster, 2000.

Ames, Charles Edward. *Pioneering the Union Pacific: A Reappraisal of the Builders of the Railroad*. New York: Appleton-Century-Crofts, 1969.

Bain, David Howard. *Empire Express: Building the First Transcontinental Railroad*. New York: Viking, 1999.

Galloway, John Debo. *The First Transcontinental Railroad: Central Pacific, Union Pacific*. New York: Simon-Boardman, 1950.

Howard, Robert West. *The Great Iron Trail: The Story of the First Transcontinental Railroad*. New York: Bonanza Books, 1962.

Lewis, Oscar. *The Big Four: The Story of Huntington, Stanford, Hopkins, and Crocker*. New York: Alfred A. Knopf, 1938.

Further Reading

BOOKS

Bracken, Jeanne Minn. *Iron Horses Across America*. Carlisle, Mass.: Discovery Enterprises, 1995.

Gordon, Sarah. *Passage to Union: How the Railroads Transformed American Life, 1829–1929*. Chicago: Ivan Dee, 1996.

Jensen, Oliver. *The American Heritage History of Railroads in America*. New York: American Heritage Publishing, 1975.

Lavender, David. *The Great Persuader*. Garden City, N.Y.: Doubleday, 1970.

Stewart, John J. *The Iron Trail to the Golden Spike*. New York: Meadow Lark Press, 1994.

Williams, John Hoyt. *A Great and Shining Road: The Epic Story of the Transcontinental Railroad*. New York: Times Books, 1988.

WEB SITES

Congress and the American West: The Transcontinental Railroad

http://www.archives.gov/exhibits/treasures_of_congress/page_15.html

Central Pacific Railroad Photographic History

http://www.cprr.org/

Pacific Railway Act

http://www.loc.gov/rr/program/bib/ourdocs/PacificRail.html

Golden Spike National Historic Site

http://www.nps.gov/gosp/

The American Experience Transcontinental Railroad Film Resource Page

http://www.pbs.org/wgbh/amex/tcrr/

Union Pacific Railroad Corporate Web Site

http://www.up.com/

PICTURE CREDITS

INDEX

About the Author

EDWARD J. RENEHAN JR., is the author of *Dark Genius of Wall Street*, *The Kennedys at War*, *The Lion's Pride*, *The Secret Six*, and *John Burroughs: An American Naturalist*. Renehan has appeared on C-SPAN, the History Channel, and PBS. He contributes to *American Heritage* and other national publications, and lives in coastal Rhode Island with his wife and two children.